Waldorf Henry Phillips

The World to Blame

A Novel

Waldorf Henry Phillips

The World to Blame
A Novel

ISBN/EAN: 9783744717687

Printed in Europe, USA, Canada, Australia, Japan

Cover: Foto ©Thomas Meinert / pixelio.de

More available books at **www.hansebooks.com**

THE WORLD TO BLAME.

THE WORLD TO BLAME.

A Novel.

BY

WALDORF H. PHILLIPS,

AUTHOR OF "AT THE MINES," "WHAT DO YOU THINK OF HIM?" ETC., ETC., ETC.

PHILADELPHIA:
CLAXTON, REMSEN & HAFFELFINGER,
624, 626 & 628 MARKET STREET.
1874.

J. FAGAN & SON,
STEREOTYPERS, PHILAD'A.

TO

Them I Hold most Dear.

GRATEFUL TO MY GOD, THAT

HE HAS BLESSED ME

WITH SUCH A

FATHER AND MOTHER.

CONTENTS.

THE
WORLD TO BLAME.

CHAPTER I.

LESLIE WYNDHAM.

AT the age of thirty-five, Leslie Wyndham had earned for himself a name and a moderate fortune. He was a fine-looking man, with eyes large and black, which seemed to read your very thoughts at a glance; hair of the same hue; the form of an Apollo; a high, intellectual forehead, (though a high forehead is not always a sign of intellectuality,) and, altogether, of a very prepossessing appearance. His manners were mild and winning, his mind well stored with knowledge, firm and well balanced, and himself cultivated, gentlemanly, courteous, and brilliant.

There was an indefinable something attractive about him. Intellect shone in his eyes. He thought quickly and deeply, but not over-hastily, weighing well this and that.

He was upright; his temper passionate, but under his control; his sympathy easily aroused;—in short, a man who had seen a great deal of the good and bad of this world; one acquainted with its curious ways and

2

passions; a man who, though yet young, had had a vast experience.

And here we may be allowed to remark, that age does not necessarily bring with it either wisdom or experience.   One may pass through multitudes of vicissitudes, and yet, really, have no experience.

The boy of fifteen may have more experience, and greater knowledge of the world and its passions, than the man of sixty, though he, personally, has seen nothing of life, while the man has passed through all its troubles, griefs, and joys.

It is observation which is experience.

The boy of fifteen, who observes narrowly the mysterious and crazy drama of life going on around him, has more true experience than the man of sixty, who has come in contact with the rough and pleasant sides of life, — who has passed through the giddy whirlpool without observing what was taking place about him.

Observation, we repeat, is really experience.

By profession, Leslie Wyndham was a journalist. He was the author of several celebrated works.   He had been the War Correspondent, during the Crimean War, of one of the best and most influential daily papers published in Gotham, and at the age of thirty-five, was one of its strongest pillars.

He was a widower.   He had, as he thought all men should do, married young, and his wife had died in giving birth to his only child, a smart boy of sixteen years, who lived with his mother's relatives in the Bay State.   Once a month regularly, Leslie Wyndham met his son and passed two or three days with him; and then came an affectionate parting on both sides.

Wyndham had no settled residence, but when in New York, he resided with a Mrs. Crosswell.

Mrs. Crosswell was a widow, and the virtues of the "late departed" were always before her eyes. She kept a private boarding-house, though not for the sake of "company," merely.

Here he found a field for character-study. There was Mr. Sniggins, who, figuratively speaking, always turned up his nose at the table, while his wife eyed everything suspiciously; Mr. Fine, who imagined himself *fine*-r and better than any one else, (his board bill was not punctually settled;) the duplex Mr. Smith, — Christian name John, — and others.

It was at Mrs. Crosswell's that Leslie Wyndham met the woman who was to have such an influence on his after life. He had been there some two successive months, before, in answer to an advertisement, a gentleman applied for board and lodging for himself and wife.

"A newly-married couple," announced Mrs. Crosswell, confidentially, at the table.

"When are they coming?" asked a rather wild young lady.

"To-morrow morning, Mrs. Pentham," replied the landlady.

"Oh, my!" with a sigh, "I suppose we'll have to be on our good behavior for a week!" said Mrs. Pentham, demurely.

Mrs. Pentham was the life of Mrs. Crosswell's house.

"Such a wild, lively, full-of-spirits, enchanting married woman, I never did see," the landlady had remarked to Leslie Wyndham.

"A little too wild for a married woman," thought Mr. Wyndham, after a few days' observance of her.

Leslie Wyndham met the newly-married couple at the dinner-table the following evening, and was duly introduced to Mr. and Mrs. Farly.

Mr. Farly was a man of prepossessing appearance, well educated, and well versed on all the topics of the day; by occupation, a stock broker.

Mrs. Farly was about eighteen years of age, with deep black eyes, handsome features, and slender form; in short, a beautiful woman. Her conversation was fascinating, attractive, and full of sound common sense; — a rather strange thing in a woman, especially of her age.

Leslie Wyndham was a good judge of character, and what he thought of Mrs. Farly and her husband, can best be inferred from the following extracts from his private diary: —

" ... A man of weak mind; one who would easily give way under the slightest misfortune, and seek oblivion in drink. A man of strong and uncontrolled passions. One who, persuaded that he had been wronged, would rush blindly into crime, to be revenged. A bad temper; easily influenced by others. He has quarrelled with his wife already. Jealous. In a bad business."

Mrs. Farly: —

" A smart, intelligent woman, of great strength of mind. Virtuous and innocent. Not as happy as she seems. Thinks she loves her husband, but is not well mated."

*   *   *   *   *   *   *

Leslie Wyndham occupied the adjoining room to that of Mr. and Mrs. Farly.

Before a month had passed, he was on familiar terms with the lady. For her husband he experienced a sort of indefinable repugnance.

His opinion of the two remained unchanged.

And so six uneventful months winged their rapid flight, and were lost in the depths of the ocean of Time. But as they were the beginning of the eventual days, we shall endeavor to review them in as few words and short a space as possible.

The journalist's opinion of Mr. and Mrs. Farly, — the new boarders no longer, — we have said remained the same; but the more he had seen of the lady, the more he had been strongly reminded of his dead wife, who had long been sleeping in her grave, but never forgotten. He tried not to think of Mrs. Farly, when he found that he began to feel an attachment for her. She was a married woman, and he must not forget that she could never be anything more to him than a friend. But Leslie Wyndham was, after all, only human; he was possessed of the same passions and emotions as the rest of us poor mortals. If Mrs. Farly could never be anything to him, he could, nevertheless, and, what is more, he did, love her.

He struggled with this passion as only a strong man with upright feelings, can struggle. He knew very well that it was a mad, wrong passion, but he could not help it. He tried not to own even to himself that he felt anything stronger than friendship for her; yet, he did.

He feared for her. Her husband was a man of

2 *   B

strong passions, fierce and vindictive in his nature, though that nature was inherently weak. Suppose some reverse should overtake him? What was more probable? He was a stock broker; he would become a speculator, if he was not one already.

Speculation is like the serpent; it fascinates while it destroys.

Leslie Wyndham could see that Mr. and Mrs. Farly's were not temperaments suited to each other.

He loved her! He found it out in a very short time. If he could not be to her anything but a friend, he could watch over, and, if chance offered, aid her.

And how were the husband and wife getting along together during these six months?

She liked the journalist; he did not. He was, we have said, of a very jealous disposition.

For the first three months they were happy. Then, alas, came little quarrels. Mary Farly could ill brook her husband's domineering manner, his little petty jealousies. She could not be his slave. If she spoke to a gentleman for an hour, her husband talked to her about it. He often spoke to her about Leslie Wyndham; he did not like to see her so much in his company. He could see nothing in a man like Wyndham, however interesting Mrs. Farly might find him.

Such jealous dispositions as James Farly's, are not, unfortunately, exceptional; and a wife, it matters not how good she may be, — and especially if she was, like Mary Farly, intellectual and high spirited, — cannot always refrain from speaking out her opinions of her husband; cannot bear to be domineered over.

Between husband and wife there should exist perfect love, harmony, and trust.

It had not been a good match. Two such differently constituted persons could not well agree together.

They quarrelled! This was the beginning:

Leslie Wyndham had spent the evening at home. They were all congregated in Mrs. Crosswell's sitting-room, a favorite place of resort after the dinner was over.

Mrs. Crosswell herself, Mr. Sniggins, lively Mrs. Pentham, and James Farly, sat round the card-table playing whist.

Leslie Wyndham, who did not, or but seldom, touch cards, and Mrs. Farly sat apart talking and laughing together.

A man like Wyndham could not fail to interest a woman like Mrs. Farly. He spoke of literature, art, music, and the drama, — subjects peculiarly attractive to her.

James Farly ever and anon cast a glance over at them. He did not like to see them so conversant with each other.

Mrs. Pentham rallied him on his play.

"Why, Mr. Farly, what are you doing? You're playing awful! You don't pay any attention at all to the game! Come, wake up! Play right!"

He murmured something. He was growing restless and uneasy. His jealous disposition gave him little peace. He longed to speak out, but he could not before "everybody." But he was glad when the game came to an end.

"Why, Mr. Farly, tired already? What, ain't you going to play another game? What ails you?"

"I can't play to-night," he replied; "I don't feel

like it. My mind wanders from the cards, and I'd
rather not play. Besides, I have had a very busy day,
and feel tired out. Good-night, all. Ready, Mary?"

"In one minute, James."

"All right; I'm going up. Be up soon," he said,
and hastily left the room.

He felt that if he remained there much longer he
must speak out; he could not control his passion. It
was gnawing at his very vitals.

"Oh," thought Mrs. Pentham, "he is jealous!
That's right! He'd like that woman to be his slave!
I'd teach him if he was *my* husband! I'd flirt just
as much as I pleased!"

It was full half an hour before Mrs. Farly ascended
to her room. Her husband was seated in the arm-
chair before the fire, his head resting on his hand.
He had not recovered from his jealous fit; he was
waiting for his wife to vent his anger.

"Well, James," she began. She was going to ask
him if he was ill, but he interrupted her.

"You've come up at last!"

There was nothing in the words themselves, but it
was the tone, the manner in which they were spoken.

"What do you mean, James?" she asked.

"I just wanted to know if you had finished your
interesting conversation with that puppy, Wyndham,"
he said, sneeringly.

The words stung her to the quick, touched her pride,
and aroused her indignation.

"James Farly," she cried, "you shall not insult Mr.
Wyndham and myself in that manner. I will not
listen to it."

" ' Mr. Wyndham and myself,' " he repeated, mockingly. "That's right! *I* was only made to support
you while you enjoyed yourself in other men's company! *I* was only made to trouble, to toil, to wear
my life out, that you might amuse yourself! *I*—"

The hot blood rushed to her face, and suffused her
cheeks. Her eyes flashed with indignation, as she cut
him short.

"Stop!" she cried. "You shall not insult me in
this manner! You shall not!"

His passion was fast getting the better of him.

"And I will not have you talk to that man!" he
said, passionately. "I expressly forbid you to! I
will not stand it, I tell you! You must behave yourself as my wife should! You shall not disgrace my
name!"

Again the hot blood rushed to her face. If she had
any bad quality, it was pride.

She spoke angrily.

"I will talk to whom I please, and when I please,"
she said. "I am not your slave, Mr. Farly, to be
commanded what to do, and what not to do! I will
not be insulted by my husband! You must treat me
with proper respect, or I will not speak to you! I
wish I had never seen you! Oh, why, why did I
marry you?"

"Beware!" he cried, threateningly, half rising from
the chair.

"That's right, coward that you are! Threaten me,
strike me, like the man that you are! I loathe you!
I despise you, with your mean little jealousies!"

She repented the words the minute she had spoken
them.

He buried his face in his hands, with a look no pen can picture! One little word then, would have made love reign again.

But, no! She would not speak that word. He, her husband, placed no faith, no trust in her. It was all his fault, she argued.

Ah! they were both in fault; but pride, cursed pride, would not allow them to acknowledge it.

"Enough!" he said, chokingly. "We know each other now. In public, we must appear—"

He could not say the word. It stuck in his throat. *She loathed him!*

He arose. He was on fire. There was murder at his heart.

He left the room, hurriedly.. He must go out into the fresh air where he could breathe.

When he had gone, she fell into a chair and wept.

"Why did he not speak?" she moaned.

Each had been waiting for the other to speak that one word, and — it had remained unsaid.

She went to bed, but not to sleep.

It was very late when he came in, and cast himself, without undressing, on the sofa.

There was little rest for either of them that night, for he, too, was uneasy and dissatisfied with himself.

CHAPTER II.

THE FIRST CURSE — JEALOUSY.

THIS quarrel ended, of course, in a reconciliation; but it left its effects. After this, they both felt that the dream had ended; that they could not be to each other again, what they had been.

Frequently, angry words passed between them. Mr. Farly spent his evenings out; Leslie Wyndham at home.

The journalist thought that he should go away from this house, but he could not. He saw that there had been a quarrel between the husband and wife; he, alone, noted the little differences in them, and instinctively felt that he was the cause of the change.

Mrs. Farly was becoming dearer to him. In the absence of her husband, she was almost constantly in his company.

And so the six months had passed.

We have said that James Farly spent his evenings away from his home.

He considered himself a misused man. He looked on Leslie Wyndham as the cause of the estrangement between him and his wife, and he *hated* the journalist.

Such men as James Farly, when in his position, or similar ones, take to drink.

James Farly lingered around hotels and bar-rooms. He essayed to drown his thoughts in fiery liquor, but he had not, as yet, become so debased as to go to his home in a state of intoxication.

There were times when he felt ashamed of himself.

One night, or, rather, evening, he arrived home, tired, sullen, and morose.

There had been a great agitation in the market that day, and every one conversant with stocks, foresaw a panic.

He did not speak to any one, nor appear at the dinner-table; his wife excused him.

She questioned him as to what was the matter with him. She did not like to see him in his present state of mind.

He did not answer her, except by a sharp, " Don't bother me! I have enough to trouble me, without *you* annoying me."

She did not question him further.

He went out early, and it was late when he returned. He had been imbibing heavily, and, though she was awake in bed when he came into the room, she pretended to be asleep.

He did not speak, but muttered to himself. She could smell the liquor in his breath. It disgusted and sickened her.

He fell asleep in the arm-chair, and his deep, hard breathing, alone broke the silence.

She could not sleep. Need we say it? She was afraid of him in his present state. Her pillow was bedewed with hot, scalding tears.

Oh! what misery to be tied for life to such a man! She compared him with Leslie Wyndham, to the latter's great advantage.

Towards morning, she fell into a doze, and when she awoke, he had already left the house.

How she passed the day can be imagined. She moved about mechanically, but her thoughts were far away from herself. She remained at home, restless and heavy-hearted.

It was a very busy day in the stock market. There was a panic. Stocks rose rapidly, which before had sold at less than par, and those which had been considered of the greatest value, and the most secure for investment, suddenly declined.

Men ran around wild, distracted, trying to cover their losses, and keep a firm footing. Such an exciting day had never been witnessed in the Stock Exchange.

James Farly came home late, after the dinner hour, and hurried to his room, looking entirely demented.

His wife was in the room, but for some minutes he said not a word to her, but, casting himself recklessly into a chair, buried his face in his hands, and for a long time sat in this attitude of dejection, staring ruin in the face.

He was deliberating how to break the terrible news to her. His jealousy was, for the time being, forgotten.

Suddenly, he raised his head and spoke.

"Mary, I have something to tell you."

She came to his side, and said gently:

"What is it? You are troubled."

"I am afraid you cannot bear up under it," he said. "It has been a very busy and exciting day. At one time I thought I would have gone crazy. You know," (she did *not* know,) "I have dabbled considerably in stocks lately. The market has greatly fallen to-day, and unless there is a change, we are—"

"Ruined!" she said, calmly.

3

"Ruined!" he repeated.

*   *   *   *   *   *   *

They passed the evening in their own room. For the first time in a long while, James Farly remained at home.

What they said can better be imagined than described.

It is better never to have wealth, than to have it and lose it.

*   *   *   *   *   *   *

The following morning, Farly was at his office very early, and his wife passed the day in nervous expectation and anxiety.

Leslie Wyndham reached his home at five o'clock that afternoon, and stopped at her room door to converse with her.

She sat in the rocking-chair by the window.

In his character of journalist it had been Leslie Wyndham's duty to record the events of the Wall street panic, and among the list of failures, he had that day been compelled to place the name of

"*James Farly.*"

He refrained carefully from mentioning the subject at all, and she, though wishing, yet not daring to, did not question him in regard to it.

While thus engaged in trivial conversation, the hall door opened and closed, and a man's heavy footstep ascended the stairs.

This man was James Farly.

His head was bent, and he half crazed by the heavy blow which had fallen on him that day.

As he reached his room door, his eyes fell on Leslie

Wyndham, an angry scowl convulsed his features, and he walked into the room with an unsteady step, trembling with passion, and, without a word, slammed the door to in the journalist's face.

Wyndham paid no attention to the rude action. He knew full well the opinion James Farly had of him; so he went into his own apartment, adjoining theirs.

He could hear their voices in angry dispute, and judged of the scene passing in their room.

Once or twice he heard his own name mentioned, and before his eye he saw a jealous, half-crazed, torn-with-passion man, and a gentle, though proud and spirited woman.

He longed to go into her room and take her part, but his good sense restrained him from obeying the impulse.

He passed the evening in his own apartment, and Mary Farly remained up stairs, also.

Her husband had left her in anger, and, fearing for his safety, she remained up waiting for him.

The weary hours passed. The clock on the mantel struck the hour of one, when she heard him open the house door.

With the exception of Mary Farly and Leslie Wyndham, the house was wrapped in slumber.

He came staggering up the stairs, the fumes of his liquor-laden breath pervading the hall and stairway. He staggered into the room in a beastly state of intoxication.

Leslie Wyndham heard him, and listened intently.

Mary Farly shuddered with inexpressible loathing, as she saw her husband.

"Up, eh? (hic,)" he said loudly.

"'Sh! You'll wake the whole house up, if you talk so loud," she said in a low tone.

"And who cares if I do?" he hiccoughed.

"I do!" she said. "If you have lost all respect for yourself, and all your sense of shame, I have not. I do not care that my husband should be seen in his present condition."

"And whose fault is it, eh?"

"Your own."

"You lie! woman. It is yours, and your paramour's, Wyndham!"

The hot blood leapt wildly through her veins; her bosom heaved with indignation, and her whole frame shook with anger, and a sense of gross injustice. But she controlled her passion by a mighty effort, and said calmly: —

"James Farly, you know not what you say. Were you sober, I would make you take those words back; as it is—"

"It's the truth, eh?" he hiccoughed, angrily.

"You lie!"

She could not keep the words back. They burst from her pale lips spontaneously.

"What!" he cried. "How dare you say that to me?"

He arose, sobered, from the chair he had fallen into, as he spoke.

Leslie Wyndham could not restrain himself any longer. He had heard every word they had spoken.

He went out of his room, and opened and closed their door quietly, without their noticing him.

James Farly stood over his wife with uplifted arm, and clenched fist, ready to strike her.

All his sense of manliness rebelled at the sight, and with a spring, the journalist rushed between the two, and caught the descending arm.

"*Coward!*" he said, and there was a world of intense loathing in the one word.

In an instant, James Farly became perfectly sober.

Again this man had come between him and his wife!

*   *   *   *   *   *   *

Neither of the trio slept that night.

They met the next morning at the breakfast-table, but not a word passed between them.

That was the last time they ever met together in Mrs. Crosswell's house.

Mr. and Mrs. Farly had come there happy; they left there that day, miserable.

What was to be the end?

CHAPTER III.

THE OTHER CURSE — DRINK.

WHAT was to be the end? What was the end? It can be told in a few words, if the reader has not already guessed it.

James Farly's descent was very rapid. The first false step, and the others quickly follow. It is very easy to descend the ladder.

His wife still remained with him, though her load seemed greater than she could bear. She worked hard with her needle for the little pittance that supported her.

Oh, it is bitter for one accustomed to the luxuries of life to live in poverty!

With the exception of Leslie Wyndham, all her friends (?) had deserted her.

James Farly, now that he had lost his fortune, had no friends but those he made in the bar-room. All his earnings went for drink.

He came home, every night, to their little garret, in the same beastly state of intoxication.

This could not last long. His wife had not entirely ceased to love him, but she could not bear to live with him in his present condition.

For two nights, in company with the journalist, she followed him, and saw him, with what feelings God alone knew, enter a notorious house of prostitution.

It was then that Leslie Wyndham begged her to procure a divorce. He would aid her. It was not right that she should be compelled to live with a man like the one she called her husband.

She could procure a divorce; and, as she had determined not to accept of any charity, but to work for her living, he would secure her a nice, quiet place as governess in a family of his acquaintance, who resided in the country, where she could live in peace.

What could be the result?

"Put yourself in her place."

On one side was a life of poverty, with a drunkard for a husband. On the other hand, a good home was offered her by a man whom she knew loved her, and whom she liked and admired.

Oh, it was a hard and bitter struggle!

It took her a long time to decide, though the life she was leading was unbearable.

Rum and liquor have worked more ruin and done more harm than all the armies the world ever saw.

Rum! the curse of civilization; the destroyer of the body and the mind; the serpent of the home circle; the agent of the devil!

The cause of nine-tenths of the murders, and divorces, and tragedies daily taking place, can be traced to this satanic agent.

Curse upon curse have been heaped upon its head, and still it goes on destroying whatever it touches, laying its blighting hand upon father, brother, and husband; dealing in death in its most agonizing form; leaving destruction and desolation along its triumphant way; striking at the very roots of earthly happiness; tempting and alluring with false hopes and promises; consoling while destroying, — the worst enemy of mankind, — the very spirit of HELL on earth!

* * * * * * *

James Farly came home one night, in his usual beastly state of intoxication.

No wife awaited him; no one welcomed him.

He waited and waited, after sleeping off his drunkenness.

He searched for the woman he called wife.

Without avail!

Only a short note on the rickety table, directed in a trembling hand to him, rewarded his search.

It was very, very short.   All it said was:

Farewell!   God forgive me and bless and reform you!   Farewell!   MARY.

He read it over a dozen times.   He could not understand it.

For some time after its full meaning burst upon his mind in all its terrible significance, he sat perfectly motionless.

There was a dull feeling at his heart; his brain whirled, and a terrible sense of loneliness came over him.

There he sat, as motionless as a statue, benumbed and half-paralyzed under this last fearful blow; under this last ruin, which he, himself, had erected with his own hands, and which had tumbled over his head,—sat in mute anguish and looked upon the ruin, — the ruin which rum and jealousy had caused.

Oh ! these two are mighty powerful and destructive agents singly ! But now they had been combined ! They had worked hard together for a human soul, and conquered !

That soul was theirs !

CHAPTER IV.

FATHER AND SON.

IN one of the most fashionable and populous streets in the Empire City, there stood a magnificent four-story-brown stone house. Imposing as its exterior undoubtedly was, its interior was no less luxurious and beautiful.

And this large and magnificent mansion, with all its wealth of furniture, pictures, etc., was occupied by two men solely, if we except the five servants who took care of it.

These two men were Leslie Wyndham and his son Frederick.

During these last six years, Leslie Wyndham had amassed wealth very rapidly; everything he touched seemed to turn into gold.

He had also been married. It was on the occasion of his second marriage that he had purchased the fine residence we have mentioned, and, having sent for his son, who at that time was in his nineteenth year, settled down into private life, bestowing charity wherever he thought it deserving, and earning the name of a true philanthropist.

But again he had the misfortune to lose his wife, three years before we re-introduce him to your notice.

He is sitting in his room, by the side of an elegant marble table, on which stands a drop light, vainly endeavoring to read the evening paper. His thoughts

C

are not on the news of the day, but on one dear, very dear to him; one to whom he feels he must soon address words of reproach, — his son.

It was with only such feelings and emotions as a true father, — a father who loved his son as Leslie Wyndham loved his, — can know, that he had watched the dissipated life Frederick had been leading.

Out every night until late in the morning, spending money freely and not in the best of ways, it was no wonder that Frederick Wyndham's name was frequently mentioned in connection with reports that, to say the least, did not do him much credit.

In fact, the young man seemed to be undoubtedly "fast," in the general acceptation of that term; and though he loved his father truly and devotedly, still the many counsels, and warnings, and lectures, as he was wont to call them, which that father had given him, were all apparently unheeded, for Frederick had got into bad company.

He was known to gamblers and licentiates; he associated with "sports," who flattered and praised him, who called him a jolly good fellow, and a " regular brick, you bet;" who tickled his vanity, and would continue to do so as long as he had the wherewithal to spend for their amusement.

He had got into bad company whom he found it very hard to shake off. They clung to him like leeches, and he was too afraid of their ridicule to tell them what the "Governor" said.

When a man is ashamed and afraid of the ridicule of those who feed upon his generosity, the natural conclusion would seem to be that he has fallen pretty low.

So, when a servant told him that his father wished to see him before he left the house, Frederick knew what was coming, and prepared himself for another "lecture."

Leslie Wyndham was pacing up and down his room with unsteady steps, when his son entered. He bade him be seated, and, seating himself, for some minutes remained silent, while the young man, with an inward feeling of unquiet and unrest, thought, "Why don't he speak and be done with it?"

Frederick was a very fine-looking young man; but the marks of dissipation were engraven on his face, and more especially around his eyes.

The feelings which agitated Leslie Wyndham cannot be described; it pained him greatly to speak harshly to his son.

Ah! they who envied him little thought that he could be, and was, very unhappy.

It was the son who opened the conversation, though not without a guilty twinge of conscience at the part he was playing.

"John told me you wished to see me," he said. "What do you want of me, father?"

"Frederick," said his father, solemnly, striving to hide his emotion, "cannot you guess what I wish of you?"

The young man moved uneasily in his chair.

"Frederick, you are young and inexperienced, and still you do not heed my counsels and my advice. Believe me, my son, — for, though you were as old as Methuselah, you would still be my son, — it is as painful for me to be compelled to reproach you, as it

possibly can be for you to listen to me. Take my
advice, — the advice of one who has passed through
the giddy whirlpool and maelstrom of life, Frederick.
Marry, and settle down; give up the life you are leading, for it can only end in your ruin."

His voice trembled, and tears were in his eyes, which
he could not suppress.

"Father," answered the son, "you know I would
not do anything wrong."

"No, no, my son, I believe you; not intentionally.
But our passions oft get the better of us. Oh, Frederick, Frederick, you would not embitter my old age,
and make my path to the grave a path of thorns!"

He gave way; broke down completely beneath his
emotion.

Silence, broken alone by his sobs, reigned for a few
moments.

Leslie Wyndham calmed himself, and continued:

"You are about to go out again, Frederick. Remain home for my sake, my son; remain home, I beg
of you. Oh, if you try, only try once to break away
from the fascination of smiling pleasures, which conceal in their gaudy exterior their hidden blackness,
you will soon rejoice that you have followed my advice; you will learn to love home as the dearest,
sweetest spot on earth, where true happiness can only
be found. There is no place like a true home, my son.
Oh, that we should be so disregardless of it! Few
people know what it is to have a true home. No one
can fully appreciate its blessings. Then do not go out,
my son, but stay and pass the night with me."

Ah! could he have only foreseen a little way ahead of

him; could he have seen the misery, the anguish of mind his answer was to cause him, he would not have said as he did say:

"I have an important engagement to-night, father, which I cannot break. After to-night I promise you faithfully and honestly, father, to follow your counsel, for I know you love me, though I am so unworthy of your love. I have been ungrateful and blind, but I shall be so no longer."

And so he went out. Had he remained at home there might have been no occasion to write this sad history.

And Leslie Wyndham was satisfied and contented. He believed his son would do as he had promised him — "after to-night."

We are so blind, O God, in our present security!

CHAPTER V.

MARY FARLY'S HOME.

AND now it becomes necessary that we take a cursory glance at Mary Farly.

In the home of Mr. and Mrs. Smithson, the friends of Leslie Wyndham, where he had procured her a situation as governess, she was made as happy and comfortable as it was possible for her to be, with the shadow of her past life ever before her eyes.

Leslie Wyndham had confided to his friend, Smith-

4

son, the history of Mary Farly's life so far as he knew
it, and so, though nominally governess, she was treated
like one of the family; and had it not been for the
bitter memories of the past, the unhappy past, which
could not be blotted out, she might have been perfectly
contented.

Mr. and Mrs. Smithson were plain, unpretentious
people. They resided in M——, a country town not
very far from New York.

The house was a fine country residence, surrounded
by spacious and elegantly laid out grounds, and ivy
and evergreens clambered up its walls.

Their married life had been very happy, and at the
time Mary Farly first entered their household, their
family consisted of a girl and boy, aged respectively
eleven and nine.

Mary Farly found her charges very easy to manage,
and apt to learn, so that her work, if such it might be
called, was light.

And so the six years had passed, with an occasional
visit from Leslie Wyndham, without any special important events.

And though the heir and daughter of the house had
grown up, still Mary Farly, at the request of the entire
family, remained, and was made to feel that she was
not dependent. Otherwise she assuredly would have
left them, for, though pride and poverty do not well
agree together, and never did or will, yet poor people
are apt to be proud as well as the rich, for they, too,
are only human.

*   *   *   *   *   *   *

Directly opposite Leslie Wyndham's residence, there

stood a small brick house, which, until within one month previous to the time of the commencement of the second part of this history, had been entirely un-inhabited so far as Leslie Wyndham could remember in regard to it.

He had often noticed this house — standing in one of the most populous and fashionable streets in the city, with its time-worn shutters always closed, and its door never opened — with a great deal of curiosity. To him it was a monument of man's foolish superstition and prejudice, and he never could quite understand why people were afraid to live in it.

In fact, a murder had been committed in that house some years before. There were whispers of a "ghost in ghastly white, stained with blood," which walked the place, but which no one would ever swear to have seen except in their own morbid imaginations, and of unearthly and hollow voices that made the blood curdle in one's veins, and ringing of bells being heard at certain hours of the night when all respectable people, save the police, were supposed to be in the arms of the strictly democratic Morpheus.

To be sure these were only rumors; for, though you were told these things in the most positive manner, no one was ready to swear to the truth of them. But they had the effect, however, of frightening off pur-chasers and tenants, and the owner found his property, which he himself would not inhabit, a burden on his hands, and one, too, that he had to pay for; for though the house was haunted, taxes had to be paid all the same. So, when an offer was made to rent the house for a couple of months, he very gladly accepted it.

Indeed, he would have allowed any one to have lived in it rent-free, could he have found a responsible party willing to do so, if merely to clear it from the suspicion of being haunted, and to prove to the outside world that there was no more danger in it than in any other house.

And so it came to pass that suddenly painters appeared upon the scene, the shutters were taken down, and new ones put up, and a general air of brightness surrounded the old deserted mansion.

The gossips began to talk and wonder who the people were who had hired the place, and the neighbors congratulated themselves on the occupancy of the haunted house.

At last the gossips were set at rest. They found out that the people who had hired this house were two middle-aged, respectable men — bachelors who were tired of boarding-houses and hotels, and who intended to keep bachelors' hall, "all by themselves."

Their names were Thomas Castle and Philip Marton, and rumor (fickle jade!) had it that they were immensely wealthy, and moved in the first circles; also that Philip Marton had all to say, or, in other words, that Castle was the slave of Marton's will.

Undoubtedly they proved quiet neighbors; no one saw them leave or enter the house; they seemed to have no business to attend to, and they made no acquaintances, and, after the usual nine days' wonder had elapsed, no one thought or troubled themselves about these two men.

The scene about to be related took place a week previous to the night when Leslie Wyndham and his son had the conversation before recorded.

The two gentlemen, Philip Marton and Thomas Castle, sat in the back extension-room, on the parlor floor of the haunted house. A cheerful fire burned in the grate, and on the small table by which they sat, facing each other, and smoking, was a decanter and two glasses. A small diagram was also on it before Marton.

It was observable that Castle drank copiously of the wine, while his companion scarcely touched his glass.

They were engaged in conversation.

"It was a lucky day for you when you met me," Marton was saying.

"And for you, too," retorted Castle

"Well, never mind about that," returned the other. "You have your revenge to satisfy, and I — well, I want money. This sort of thing is getting played out. It's all very nice, but it don't pay, and consequently can't last long now. So we must to work soon, and the sooner the better."

"But the danger," whispered the other, uneasily.

"What a cowardly chicken you are!" exclaimed Marton, in undisguised contempt. "The danger? Why, man, what do you mean? What danger? There is absolutely none at all! Just leave all that to me. Do as I bid you, and everything will come out all right. Depend upon me, and do as I tell you — nothing more or less."

"I do leave it all to you, Marton; you know I do. You beat the devil at plotting, and I confess there are times when I wonder whether you really are a man —"

"Or fiend," interrupted the other. "Thank you," he continued, sarcastically; "you are complimentary—

4 *

very complimentary, indeed.   But so long as you have
such a high opinion of me, and consent to follow my
directions, why, all right."

"You know well enough, Philip Marton, that I
would do anything to have my revenge, without —"

"Risking your own safety."

"Revenge! Revenge! Revenge! By day I think
of it, and night after night my dreams are all of
vengeance! Revenge on the man who blasted my
happiness, and ruined my life, and made me the des-
picable wretch that I am."

"And I am showing you the means by which you
can satisfy your passion; I am opening a path for you.
And not only that — not only do you satisfy your thirst
for vengeance, but you also get remunerated for all that
you have suffered. Now, first, as to the divorce. We
have seen the record of that. He did not obtain it
here; he was too wise to try that. He took her where
a divorce could be procured with less trouble, and
little, if any, publicity. Then he married her secretly;
I feel positive of that. That accounts for their not
living together, but he sees her. Wherever the devil
she is, I can't find out. If she has changed as much
in the last six years as you have, Castle, her own mother, if the worthy lady was living, would not be able
to recognize her. Being his wife, then, and he being
rich as Crœsus, or any other man, at his death she will
come in for his stamps, etc."

"But if he has made a will?"

"In favor of the other one, you mean? What if
he has? All his relatives are dead, with that exception. Now suppose, for instance, the other one —"

"You don't mean —"

"Never mind what I mean. Leave me to fix all that. Philip Marton never fails in his plans. Once she inherits his wealth, we can easily have the divorce set aside, and then we are all right."

"But the danger."

"Still harping on the same old thing! I tell you there is none at all. Why, man, I have seen the same case on trial, and what was the result? Why, everybody said he was right; public opinion was in his favor: the press sustained him, and he came off quite a hero!"

He laughed as he thought of that scene. He saw it all before him. The court-room was the theater where the comedy was played. He saw all the actors, "in his mind's eye, Horatio:" the lawyers, the audience, the judge, jury, and the poor, persecuted, innocent mur—! What a mockery of justice that was!

It was no wonder that he laughed; it was no wonder that he did not fear after witnessing that exhibition of a burlesque on law and justice! Such a sight was not calculated to inspire one with awe — the sight of a mean, cowardly, acknowledged assassin, being declared innocent!

And Castle could not but laugh too, after Marton's recital of those facts.

"I am satisfied," he said, "you are right, Marton."

"Certainly I am. You see I have made myself acquainted with all these things. Philip Marton does not act unless he knows what he is doing. I think as much of myself as you positively can of yourself, and I am not so foolish as to put my precious head in the lion's mouth recklessly! Not much! You should know that by this time."

CHAPTER VI.

WHAT THE MORNING BROUGHT.

IT was very late when Frederick Wyndham reached his home, and opening the front door with his latch key, ascended the stairs to his apartment, on the third floor.

Coming from the cold winter's night into the warmth of the heated house sent a thrill of pleasure through him.

Remembering his conversation with the father who loved him so well, and whom he also loved, Frederick had not spent the night in drinking and gambling. He had pledged himself to renounce these evils forever; and, as a beginning, he had gone to the home of the rich and beautiful girl who loved him with all the intensity of her young heart, and who was dearer to him than all the world beside.

How beautiful and noble and pure she was in comparison with the women whom he met in his debaucheries, when rendered semi-unconscious by the arch-fiend, Drink!

He could not but feel ashamed of himself in her presence; he could not but wonder that one so pure loved him, and he so unworthy of her heart's best emotions.

The words of his father had taken root in his mind before. He had been severing, as far as it was possible, his connection with the impure beings who had been the companions of his disgraceful orgies.

This was the engagement which could not be broken, and of which he had spoken to his father.

The young man was pure and noble, and generous by nature. It was his evil companionship which had led him astray, and kept concealed the inherent goodness of his being. When his father first began talking to him of the course of life he had been leading, his senses and his finer feelings began to awake and struggle to free themselves from the unworthy chains which had kept them so long in submission.

It was slow, up-hill work, and done in secret. No one knew of the terrible battle that had been going on within his breast, between passion and vice and virtue. Virtue at last had triumphed.

He passed the evening in the company of the girl-woman who loved him, and who had all along excused his imprudencies in secret, and laid their blame to the follies and snares which beset every young man's footsteps in a great city.

His father did not dream of his intimate acquaintance with this girl; did not know of the struggle which had waged in his breast. He only heard the evil reports, and Frederick said naught in contradiction of them. He was waiting for a certain event to happen before he made an announcement to his father, which he knew would give him joy and comfort, and make him happy as regarded his son's future.

The Dervilles were old friends of Leslie Wyndham's, and Frederick had visited there very often; but the idea that May Derville was to be his son's wife had never occurred to him. He had never thought of the possibility of a match being made between the two, though nothing would have pleased him more than to have seen his son married and settled in life.

May Derville was a girl in years, but a woman in thought and feeling. She had knowledge far beyond her age. She was the personification of a true woman, and, though she had never confessed but to herself, her love for Frederick Wyndham, the young man had read her secret. Her heart spoke in the language of her soft, pitying eyes.

That night Frederick had confessed his love to her. He had told her all: his past life, hiding nothing, palliating nothing, and his resolves for the future. And she had accepted him, and they were engaged.

It was, therefore, with a light heart, beating with joy and happiness, that Frederick Wyndham wended his homeward way.

The light was out in the hall, but he knew his way up to his rooms, as well in the darkness as in the day.

As he passed his father's room, he saw that the gas, as was Leslie Wyndham's custom, was burning low in one corner, and the door was slightly ajar.

He had ascended the stairs very lightly, making as little noise as possible, but as he passed the door, his father called out:

" Is that you, Frederick?" and he answered,

" Yes, sir. Good-night."

" I would like to be awoke early, Frederick."

" All right, sir. Good-night; good-night."

Then he went up to his own apartments.

The little clock in his room struck six, as he awoke. It mattered not how late he retired, precisely at six —

not from choice, but habit — sleep left him. He did not usually arise, however, but lay awake in bed reading.

It was a dull, cloudy morning, and the sky betokened a coming snow-storm.

Recollecting the wish his father had expressed to him of being awoke early, he jumped out of the comfortable bed, and, without dressing himself, proceeded down the stai ɟ in his night-gown.

There is nothing so hard on a cold winter's morning as getting out of bed.

Dressing and undressing are two plagues in cold weather.

Leslie Wyndham slept in the hall-room, using the large one as his *sanctum sanctorum*. A safe was in this large room, in which he kept his papers.

Frederick did not notice that the gas, which had been burning when he came in, was now out.

The room was very dark, for the inside blinds were closed and barred, so that the early light of the morning could not penetrate into the room.

Frederick passed through the sanctum, but as he entered the hall-room, it felt to him as if something sticky was on his feet.

He advanced a few steps toward the bed, and was about to stretch forth his hand to touch his father, when he stumbled and fell over something cold.

A chill went through his frame, and acting on the impulse of the moment, he hastily arose, trembling with fear, and opening the blind, let the dull morning light into the room.

The sight that met his eyes, and thrilled him through

and through with horror, haunted him night and day while life lasted.

It were impossible to describe what he felt at that moment; but, with a shrill shriek, he rushed down the stairs like a madman, and regardless of the fact that he was in undress, opened the front door, and, standing on the cold steps, upon which the snow-flakes had began to fall, in his bloody feet and night gown, raised his hands, which were also covered with blood, and shouted wildly:

"MURDER! MURDER! POLICE! POLICE!"

CHAPTER VII.

AFTER THE MURDER.

THE murder of Leslie Wyndham created great excitement, because of its mysterious nature.

The news spread like wildfire. The newspapers put out bulletins, and the sole topic of conversation for the time being was of Leslie Wyndham.

Who was guilty? His son had been the last one known to enter the house; he had bade his father good-night, and been answered. The servants had all retired, and though suspicion for a time rested on one of them — a man — it was quickly cleared up, and the mystery still remained unravelled.

What was the motive? Robbery? The safe was open, and the papers had been handled and tossed about recklessly, but no money had apparently been taken, for there was money in it. Was it likely that robbers would look at the papers and not take the gold that was before their eyes? No! that was impossible!

And where are we safe, if not in our own houses? it was asked. If a man like Leslie Wyndham could be murdered in his own house, where others were sleeping, and the murderer escape without leaving a trace behind him by which he could be discovered, who could call their lives their own?

No sound had been heard during the night by any of the servants, or the murdered man's son, who slept directly above him. They all swore positively to this; and yet there were signs and evidences of a severe and bloody struggle having taken place. Must not the murderer's clothes have become stained with the blood of his victim?

The mystery was as impenetrable to mortal eyes as the heavens.

The murderer had done his work well, whoever he was. He had come and done his dastardly deed silently, and silently departed. The secret was locked up in his own breast.

Was there more than one! A heavy duty fell on the police to discover the assassin or assassins. The people looked to them for a solution of the mystery that veiled this crime.

They worked diligently and incessantly. Detectives and policemen took possession of the house, and no one was allowed to enter or leave it, except Frederick and the newspaper reporters.

In the meantime, while all this was taking place, might not the murderer have been laughing at the officers of the law, and effected his escape? Whither had he fled? It was not likely that he would remain in the same city where his crime had been committed. These were questions which no one could answer.

The coroner's inquest was held. It developed nothing new — nothing that was unknown. There was no clue to the assassin or his motive. The police were stimulated by the offer of large rewards; but they had nothing to work on. The mystery remained as black as ever. Who would dissolve it?

And so Leslie Wyndham was buried. The funeral was very large; but Frederick was not present.

The traditional nine days elapsed, and the speculation in regard to the mystery ceased. There were new and important events to engross public attention.

In a large city events which once caused great excitement are soon and easily forgotten. There is always something new and strange taking place. Event follows event with unceasing rapidity. All receive due attention, and then fall back to make way for something new.

And so, for a while, Leslie Wyndham and the mystery of his death ceased to be talked of.

Where, all this time, was Frederick Wyndham?

The shock which his system had suffered on that eventful morning, when he had tripped over the dead body of his father, had thrown him upon a bed of sickness.

By a singular fatality he had been conveyed to the residence of Mr. Derville, and here poor May had faithfully tended to him all through the fever and delirium which ensued.

Thoughts of his father were ever uppermost in his mind, and in his delirium he moaned wildly, "Father, oh, father!" He begged to be forgiven for the suffering he had caused the dead, and he recounted, with a horrible minuteness, the discovery of the murder.

While Leslie Wyndham was being conveyed to his last resting-place, his son was tossing wildly on his couch, from side to side, moaning and crying, "Father! oh, father, forgive me, forgive me! I did not mean to pain you, for I loved you — oh! I loved you!"

Then he would laugh — a shrill, piercing laugh that made the blood curdle in the veins of those who heard it — and starting up in his bed would point with his finger, and cry,

"I see him! I see him! Oh, he is killing him! Murder! murder! Police! police!" and fall back exhausted.

*   *   *   *   *   *   *

"Yes; she's a proud, stuck-up thing."

"So homely and conceited, too."

"She's no better than she ought to be, either."

"What do you mean?"

"Why, haven't you heard?"

"No."

"What! you don't know?"

"I really don't. What is it?"

"Oh, nothing! I thought you knew; but never mind."

This conversation was repeated, with additions, to some one else. Some one else added to it, and told her particular friend, who, enlarging and magnifying its importance, told her particular friend. And so, from a little spiteful conversation, a vile and horrible story was concocted. No one knew anything about it, except "They say," that convenient subterfuge for scandal-mongers. But the effect was the same. A fair woman's name was blasted forever, and she was made to feel that life was a curse, that she was shunned and despised, until, in a fit of desperation, she ended her existence.

From a little acorn springs the giant oak.

Somebody made a remark in regard to Leslie Wyndham's murder. It went around in whispers, as though the whisperers were aware of the lie they were uttering, gradually gaining ground and credence.

It was a terrible thing — a terrible charge. But by a certain class of persons it was eagerly seized, commented upon and believed.

We may divide the world into two great classes — the rich and the poor.

Among the poor, so far as regards themselves, we will find more charity, more brotherly love, and more of the helping hand. But between them and the rich there is an indefinable hatred.

Let a rich man, or a rich man's son, be accused of any crime, how quick the poor say, with a sneer:

"There is your rich man, your good man; that's the kind of men they are."

It was this class who hastened to believe and repeat the horrible rumor respecting Leslie Wyndham's murder, while, at the same time, they shrugged their shoulders, and said:

"He has money, though. It would be different with me."

Now there is nothing much in these words themselves, yet when uttered by the poor in certain cases, they conceal a mint of hidden meaning.

This feeling between the rich and poor is, in part, jealousy; yet the true cause of it is because the rich, (we speak of rich and poor as a class, not individually) instead of helping the poor, look down upon the common laborer with scorn, forgetting that without him they could not have their grand brown stone fronts and palaces. They do not think what they owe to this man; they forget that every man is dependent on his fellow-man. The true cause of this feeling is because the rich crush the poor. How, then, can there be any brotherly feeling between them?

Labor is dependent on capital; but capital is also dependent on labor. Neither should belittle or tyrannize the other.

But, unfortunately, as the Elizabethan era was the age of literature, the nineteenth century is more particularly the age of money-making. Everything bends the knee before the shrine of Mammon.

The lawyer, the doctor, the laborer, the business man, (again speaking of a class, and not of an individual) all pursue their different avocations. And this great object for which they work, and work, and labor, and toil, and fret, and worry, and gamble, and cheat, and rob, and lie, with such commendable, to be praised industry — this great object, after all, sifted down, amounts to — what? Not a desire to benefit their fellow-men, but to what Washington Irving has very

5 *

aptly and expressively termed the "almighty dollar!"

Asking the reader's pardon for this digression, we continue:

It must be remembered that neither Mr. Derville or Frederick knew aught, or heard aught, of these rumors. In fact, the latter was still confined to his room, with gentle May for his nurse, and neither of them saw any of the newspapers.

One fine morning, not quite a week after this rumor began to spread, Mr. and Mrs. Derville were sitting alone at breakfast, leisurely sipping their coffee, when, suddenly, he uttered an exclamation of mingled horror and surprise, and, letting the paper he was reading fall from his hands, cried, with a face as pale as death —

"It is a lie! a lie! a wicked, soulless lie?"

'Why, what is the matter?" exclaimed his wife, alarmed.

"See there!" he said, vehemently, and pointing to the paper.

She took it up and read in large letters:

LESLIE WYNDHAM'S ASSASSIN!!
DISCOVERY OF THE MURDERER!
A TERRIBLE DENOUEMENT!

Full Particulars of the Murder, and How it was Committed!

She stopped, with a feeling of coming evil at her heart.

Her husband sat perfectly motionless, his face as white as marble, and his teeth clenched tightly together.

She continued reading:

"A rumor has been going round from mouth to mouth, during the last few days, and gaining strength and ground, in regard to this mysterious tragedy, which has, thus far, puzzled and baffled all the efforts of the authorities to discover any trace of its perpetrators."

And then it went on to narrate the full particulars.

The writer pretended to know all about the tragedy. He told how the assassin had entered the house, and detailed, with a horrible minuteness, all his movements before and after perpetrating the crime, and concluded with a terrible charge that sent all the color from Mrs. Derville's face, and made her tremble with anger.

The article came out boldly, and accused Frederick Wyndham of being a parricide!

"It is false! utterly false, Richard!" she cried, "and the writer knows it, too. Oh, how can they publish such a wicked lie! Richard, Richard! it is not so! it is not so!"

"Be calm, Mary, be calm. It is too late to remedy it now. It is in print, and by this time all New York knows it. We can do nothing at present. It is a sensation, got up to sell the paper, utterly untrue, and its author shall suffer for it!"

"But what shall we do, Richard! what shall we do? Oh, it is terrible — infamous!"

"Terrible, indeed! And the man who could write such an article, without a particle of proof, is a villain, for whom hanging is too good. He shall be attended to: never fear. But we must not let them see the paper; he must know nothing of it."

By the next morning all New York had perused

the horrible narrative. It was copied into other papers, and its author denounced by them all.

There were cries of shame! terrible! wicked! disgraceful! and threats of horsewhipping, and other summary proceedings. And yet many of those who were loudest in their denunciations secretly believed it to be true.

What if it was unnatural? It was not impossible. Such things had happened more than once. And then he was known to be a wild, dissipated young man.

But the next issue of the paper increased the excitement to a fearful degree.

"We have been denounced and threatened on all sides," it said, "but we still stick to the truth, and repeat what we have said. Leslie Wyndham was murdered by his son. We are fully aware of the nature and horribleness of the charge we make; we would wish it possible that we were mistaken. But in the face of the facts, and after due consideration, we were compelled to come out boldly with the accusation, and we can prove it."

Here followed an account of Frederick Wyndham's dissipated life, his father's remonstrances, the quarrels between the two — all tending to show the young man to be utterly unprincipled. The motive alleged for the crime was — money! The safe had been searched and ransacked for Leslie Wyndham's will, which his son knew almost the same as disinherited him. In the event of the murdered man dying intestate, his vast estate would descend to his only heir-at-law — his son. Was not the motive sufficient.

The whole story was narrated coolly and calmly, supported by facts and circumstances.

The article concluded:

"The police have been negligent and careless in their investigation. Let them look in the second bureau-drawer in the parricide's room, far back, and see what they find wrapped up in a small parcel which lies there."

"The second bureau-drawer in the parricide's room!" No one had thought of looking there; but long before the paper was out on the news-stands, the drawer was searched, and the small parcel found.

Carefully, and with trembling fingers, it was opened. There were five rolls of paper wrapped around the article inside it.

This article was a razor, stained and clotted with blood, and on the handle was engraved the name "Frederick Wyndham."

* * * * * * *

One more scene, heartrending in the extreme, must be recorded before the conclusion of this chapter.

Mr. Derville had been thinking over that article in the paper for some time. By listening attentively he found that there were many who more than half believed the preposterous story.

He came to one conclusion. Frederick must leave the city until the *furore* created by that article died out.

On the very morning that the paper came out reiterating its previous story, he had a carriage waiting at his house door.

Frederick Wyndham had so far recovered as to be

able to walk about his room. He had not, as yet, ventured to go into the street. Happy, delighted May was always with him — always at home.

For a few moments after Mr. Derville entered the room, the conversation was about — well, nothing.

But at last he spoke out.

"Frederick, my son," he said, kindly, but with an air of determination, "I have a carriage waiting at the door for you. You must leave the city with me for a few days."

"Leave the city!" echoed poor May, feeling slightly alarmed.

"Leave the city?" repeated Frederick. "Why, what do you mean? What for?"

"Don't ask me any questions, for God's sake, my son, but come. Only for a few days. Come, come quick, before it is too late."

He spoke in a tone of entreaty. The young man was completely mystified. Poor little May clung to his arm.

At this instant Mrs. Derville entered hurriedly, evidently in great agitation.

"O, Richard, it is too late! too late! too late!" she cried, and falling on her knees, she hid her face in her husband's lap.

He bowed his head in terrible anguish.

Two policemen entered. One closed the door, and stood with his back to it. The other advanced, and laid his hand on the young man's shoulder.

"Come, my man," he said, "you are wanted. Your carriage is too late!"

"What do you mean?" the young man said, sternly. "What is the object of this farce?"

"I am not here to answer questions," was the reply. "I hope you'll not compel us to use force. Best come along quietly."

"Frederick! Frederick!" cried May, throwing her slight airy form between the two. "There is some mistake — some terrible mistake here!"

"There is no mistake, Miss. I wish there was — I hope there is," the officer said, kindly, touched in spite of himself by the sight of her pale, agonized face, "for your sake and his. I must perform my duty. Young man, you must come with me!"

Frederick Wyndham was struck dumb with astonishment; he could not speak.

Mr. and Mrs. Derville were silent.

"Oh! no! no! no!" cried poor May, throwing her arms around him as if to hold him fast. "You shall not take him. He shall not go. Go away. Go away. Oh! say you will let him be in peace. You will kill him. What has he done? What has he done?"

"He is charged with the murder of Leslie Wyndham, his father."

The words fell upon their ears like the knell of doom. A groan escaped Derville's lips; his wife shrieked.

"It is not true! It is not true! O God! it is not true! Frederick, Frederick, it is not true!

"It is a lie — a base lie," he murmured, hoarsely.

"Thank —— " The arms slipped from his body, and the poor girl sank unconscious to the floor.

*   *   *   *   *   *   *

The same carriage which had been provided to take him out of the city conveyed Frederick Wyndham to the Tombs.

CHAPTER VIII.

IN THE TOMBS.

THE effect of the news of Leslie Wyndham's terrible end on Mary Farly can better be imagined than described. She knew him as a man among men; as one who had been her steadfast friend in her hour of need; who had saved her, time and time again, from a husband's drunken fury; as one who loved her, whom she revered, and yet was separated from by a cruel fate. To her he was pure, good, honest, and noble; one of those men to whom the weak almost instinctively look up for protection.

It was a great blow, also, to the Smithsons, the kind friends whom Leslie Wyndham had provided for her. Knowing her as they did, they could not but respect her grief.

She would fain have gone and looked upon his loved face for the last time, ere he was placed in the narrow home that awaits us all, forever. But she could not. The stern and cruel laws of society and propriety forbade it. What would she, a stranger, want among the mourners for the dead?

She shrank from exposing her sad history to the gaze of a cold world; cold, while commiserating with that kind of lofty pity that stings the proud soul to the quick.

Yes; she was proud. What was born in her not all the tortures of the damned could have extinguished.

The poor, the miserable, are proud, as well as the rich; and that kind of pity which the rich oft express for the poor when they read of the end of some sad history, only serves to more embitter the hatred existing between the two classes. Not that Mary Farly's was that cursed lofty and foolish pride we so often meet with. By no means. She did not imagine or consider herself as far superior to all other people; gold was not her standard, but education; she judged by the beauty and nobility of the soul, not by the face and clothes.

Mr. Smithson went to attend to the funeral rites of his old friend. He was well known as Leslie Wyndham's most intimate and esteemed friend, and, by common consent, he took charge of the necessary arrangements for the funeral. So that he remained in town, leaving his family and Mary Farly to await his return, the latter in a state of nervous anxiety which words cannot express.

It was on the very day that Frederick Wyndham was arrested that he returned to his home.

To say that they were astonished and horrified at the news he brought would be but faintly to express their feelings.

Mary Farly did not exhibit a trace of the emotion she felt; but she had immediately made up her mind as to the course she should pursue.

She spoke calmly when she asked:

"And do you believe him guilty, Mr. Smithson?"

"No, never! It is utterly preposterous," he replied. "The idea was first started by an obscure paper, I know not with what motive, more than a week ago. The article was severely condemned, but the paper continued

6

to accuse the young man of being a parricide.   The
consequence is that he has been arrested.   The particulars are very contradictory at present, and the
greatest excitement prevails.   The evening papers say
that the proof against him appears to be very conclusive.   It is claimed that a bloody razor, bearing his
name, has been found in his drawer.   I have not
heard of any other evidence against him, but I am
positive that he is innocent.   It is incredible.   In the
morning I shall go to town early and see what I can
do.   I shall, therefore, in all probability not return."

"I shall go with you," Mary Farly said, quietly.

"You?"

"I.   Do not endeavor to persuade me to alter my
determination.   Please do not oppose me.   You know
what I owe to the dead."

Her voice trembled slightly here, and for a moment
her eyes were blinded by her tears, and she could not
speak.   Then she continued:

"I must see his son and judge for myself of his
innocence.   I feel that he is not guilty—and, oh! shall
I sit idle here in a turmoil of anxiety and expectation,
while his son is in danger?   You smile; you think I
can be of no help.   Oh, if I see him, if I but hear
him say that he is innocent, as I feel he is, I shall
work, work to save him, to establish his innocence.
Oh, that such a terrible charge, involving life and
death — a charge which is certain to leave a stain on
an innocent being's name should be so lightly brought,
should be made public on such slender grounds!   I
know the world.   Accuse one of a crime, and there are
always those who, even if the accused's innocence be

established, will still think him guilty. Oh, it is terrible! horrible! His son — his son a murderer! Oh, no! no! no! it is impossible! He was noble, he was good, just, pure, honest; and can they tell me, who knew him so well, that such seed could bear poisonous fruit? No! no! He is innocent — I feel it; I know it. I must see him — see him alone. I must, if need be, tell him all that I owe to his — his father, if he will not listen to me without knowing why I befriend him. Then do not oppose my wishes. I must see him."

She spoke earnestly — from her heart.

He saw that she meant what she said, and, though he would rather she would have remained where she was, after her earnest words he could not oppose her desire.

He knew more than he cared to tell. He was aware of the dissipated life the young man had been leading, and he knew how every little thing, in itself amounting to nothing, would be perverted, and made to tell against the accused. From what he had heard during the time he had remained in the city he felt that the evidence against Frederick would be terrible.

They went to the city together the following morning. What she felt, what she suffered, what her thoughts were, during that, to her, long ride, only God and herself ever knew. She did not once speak.

All around them the passengers were reading the morning papers, and speculating as to his innocence or guilt. The excitement which prevailed could be felt and seen, but not portrayed.

At last the journey was ended, and after some little trouble and necessary delay, they entered the gloomy and frowning portals of that dismal building, known as the Tombs, which so many have entered, never to emerge from again in the consciousness of liberty.

Short as had been the time since his arrest, through the kindness of his friends and the warden, the prisoner's cell had been fitted up comfortably — the papers stated " luxuriously."

He was seated near the bed, thinking, when the two entered. Though he was very pale and weak-looking, he was very calm and self-possessed, almost unnaturally so. In fact it was impossible for him to grasp or comprehend the full nature and meaning of the crime with which he was charged. He was as much in the dark as any one in the city; he could not understand his situation. It appeared to him like a horrible nightmare.

He arose as they entered, and recognizing Mr. Smithson, extended his hand, with a painful smile, saying:

" I am glad to see you, and thank you for your kindness. I have had many friends call to see me. You see they have made me as comfortable as possible, under the circumstances."

Mr. Smithson shook his hand warmly, and said, cheerfully:

" It pleases me to see that you are so calm, and that you have recovered from your sickness. Keep up a brave heart, my boy. It is all a terrible mistake, that will soon be explained satisfactorily. There are friends outside who will work for you. Be of good cheer, and keep firm; for, remember, you are innocent. That knowledge should bear you up against all the malice of your enemies."

Then, after a little desultory conversation, he introduced Mary Farly, who, standing in the background, had been scrutinizing Frederick's appearance closely.

Upon hearing her sad history, which Mr. Smithson considered it best to disclose to him, and her determination, the poor young man could not restrain for a moment his emotion, and, grasping her extended hand, murmured chokingly:

"God bless you! Oh, this is horrible! I cannot understand it at all! I am innocent! God knows I am innocent! This is terrible! This suspicion will kill me, I am sure."

"Don't give way so, my poor boy," Mr. Smithson said, cheerfully. "We all know you are innocent, and we will prove it. Only keep up a brave heart, and all will go well, depend upon it. Trust in God."

Then, saying that he would call soon again, and telling Mary to meet him at the —— Hotel, he bade the young man good-by, and left the two alone.

For some minutes after his departure they remained silent. Then, suddenly, she took his hand in hers, and looking him full in the face, said:

"Tell me again that you are innocent!"

"I am innocent!" he exclaimed, almost proudly. "Before God I swear that I am innocent. I know as much about it as you do. I am in the dark — totally in the dark — in regard to this terrible accusation. I cannot yet believe that it is a reality. Oh, God! can you doubt me?"

"No, no! a thousand times, no! You are innocent; I would venture my existence on it. Cheer up, oh! cheer up, and trust in Him who seeth even the little

6 *   E

sparrow fall. Remember that you have friends who
would die for you, willingly. It is all a mistake — a
horrible nightmare that will soon pass over. And
now, command me; tell me, is there anything I can
do for you?"

"No — yes," he answered, after a moment's hesita-
tion, striving to conquer his emotion, and succeeding.
"You are a woman. I place implicit faith in you,
though I have not known you long, for I feel that
you are my friend. You have loved, you have suffered. There is one who loves me, one whom I love, for
whom I feel more than for myself. It is the thought
of her that causes me to suffer. For myself, I am
innocent; that knowledge it is which makes me so
calm, and keeps my spirits up. But she loves me, —
I, who am so unworthy of such a pure, self-sacrificing
love. She will suffer for me. Oh, God! oh, God!
May! oh, dear May! My love! my love!"

He stopped, for his emotion was again choking him;
but presently he continued:

"Go to her; confront her as only a woman can.
Tell her that I am innocent, that all is right. Cheer
her, support her; tell her that I think of her ever;
tell her that I beg of her not to fret or worry; that it
is better I should not see her. It would unnerve
and weaken me, now when I have most need of my
strength. Tell her that night and day I pray for her;
that her image is always before my eyes to instil me
with hope and courage. I beg of her not to suffer for
me; not to give way to despair, but to hope for the
best. Tell her how calm I am. You, who are a
woman who has lived and suffered, will know how to

comfort her.   Stay; I will give you a few lines to her."

He sat himself down and wrote, while the tears stood in his eyes, and her heart went out to him in pity.   Then, when it was finished, he gave it to her and said:

"Remember what I have told you.   And now good-by; I will see you again.   Good-by, and may God bless you!"

CHAPTER IX.

TRIED FOR HIS LIFE.

THE feeling against Frederick Wyndham was, from some cause, very great and bitter.   The public mind had been excited by a series of unpunished crimes, and the public tongue clamored for vengeance.   The press, that mighty agent for good or evil, even those papers which had scouted at the idea when it was first broached, after his arrest, all denounced the parricide, as they called him.

Instead of keeping strictly to their duty, which is to record facts only, and not pronounce verdicts, all the newspapers commented upon "the horrible crime which had been perpetrated in our midst," and called the prisoner the assassin.

The law presumes all persons innocent until proved guilty; and yet Frederick Wyndham was called a murderer before his trial.   The newspapers presumed him guilty. It was wrong, very wrong, and unjust in them to influence public opinion one way or another. In times of great excitement popular opinion is hastily formed, and, as a general rule, always wrong. It is only when time has been given the public mind to ponder and reflect, and the public pulse to cool and calm, that public opinion can be justly formed; and it was time enough for the press to comment after the question of the prisoner's guilt or innocence was determined by law, and not before.

Where life or death hangs in the balance there should be no prejudice, no prejudging. The lives that have been blasted forever, and the injury which has been done through the habit of publicly prejudging and commenting on cases before they have been tried, are incalculable.

The press of a free country like the United States wields great power, possesses great influence and moulds public opinion. How important is it, then, that they should not swerve one iota from their duty? How important is it, then, that they should not judge of a fellow-being's guilt until it is proved? Is the question hard to answer? Is it not easy to perceive what an incalculable amount of harm and wrong they can do?

"Judge not lest ye be judged."

It was the day of the trial; for, despite the hopes and assurances of his friends, Frederick Wyndham had been duly indicted for the greatest crime known to the law — wilful murder.

Men fall in battle; men die every day, yet nothing is thought of it; but at the mere mention of the word "murder," what excitement springs up! Why? Because it involves the question of the people's safety.

What a host of thoughts and reflections that simple word conjures up! How terrible its significance!

The court-room was crowded to its utmost extent by a miscellaneous gathering. It was not a very large room at the best. Lawyers, reporters, and judge were there. The ablest counsel that could be procured had been retained in the prisoner's behalf. The District Attorney was on hand to look after the case for the people. It would be a great triumph for him, if he won the case. He was a man new to his office, young and able, and this was his first great case. What was it to him that a man was on trial for his life? What was it to him that the man was young and proclaimed himself innocent of the terrible crime with which he was charged, and for which he stood before the tribunal of justice to be tried for his life? Did he think of the prisoner, or did he think of the result, if he should gain a verdict on his side — in his favor? Can we blame him that all other considerations were swallowed up in the thought of that most powerful motor of human actions — self?

The prisoner sat in his seat, pale, but firm. Who could tell the suffering, the agony which he had known since his arrest and imprisonment? There he sat, weak and pale, proud and determined, the cynosure of all eyes. Was he guilty, and could he sit there thus boldly and face his accusers, or was he innocent, and was it the light of innocence which shone in his supernaturally bright eyes? His guilt or innocence would soon be determined.

Some among the crowd wavered in their opinions, while others smiled grimly, and said, " He is a deep 'un."

His counsel were by his side, cheering and encouraging him.

He kept his eyes resolutely away from wandering a short distance back of him, where sat an old man, slightly haggard, and three ladies, deeply veiled.

A strange friendship had sprung up between Mary Farly and poor May Derville.

There is no friendship so great, so pure, or so lasting as that which is formed and has its origin in a common misfortune.

A great shadow had thus early fallen on the lifepath of this loving young girl—a shadow which threatened to darken her existence for years, and perhaps forever. The other had seen and suffered, until she had become used to suffering. Her life had been blasted in its youth. She had known luxury and poverty, happiness and misery.

Ah! sometimes all the happiness of years cannot blot out or atone for the suffering of a day.

We do not intend to describe the meeting of Mary Farly and May Derville, or how they passed those terrible days before the trial, nor what a blighting effect they had on poor May. We could not if we wished, satisfactorily to ourselves or to our readers. They were sad, sad days of darkness and grief.

Poor May had lived years in a single month. Her parents and Mary tried to dissuade her from attending the trial, but vainly. She had determined to be present, to hear all the evidence and the accusations, though it killed her; and now she is here in the court-room.

But listen: the proceedings have begun. They are empanelling a jury. First one is rejected; he has formed an opinion. Then another is opposed to capital punishment. Another answers correctly, and is accepted by the prosecution; but the learned counsel for the defence think that he appears entirely too anxious to get on the jury, and in consequence challenge him peremptorily.

It is slow, tedious work; but a jury is obtained at last. See, there sit the twelve men who hold the prisoner's life in their hands. He looks on the jury, the jury look on him. The trial begins.

The District Attorney is speaking. His speech is very powerful, very able, very bitter against the prisoner.

We will not dwell upon the evidence. He proves that the prisoner has led a very dissipated life; that the razor with which the bloody deed had evidently been committed had been found in the prisoner's room, and was, in fact, his; he calls John Jones, the man-servant before referred to, who testifies that angry words and vain remonstrances had often passed between the deceased and the prisoner; that on the very night of the murder he had heard the two talking of the life the prisoner had been leading; he shows that the prisoner, by his own admission, was the last one known to enter the house, and had been the first one to discover the murder. The theory in regard to the motive, founded on the evidence, was that the deceased had made a will not in favor of the prisoner, and it was to destroy this will that the crime had been committed.

The case looked very black against the prisoner; the circumstances, to say the least, were suspicious.

The prosecution show that on the very day of the arrest a carriage had been provided by the prisoner's friends to aid in his escape.

The prosecution rest.

The court adjourns.

The prisoner is conveyed back to the Tombs.

On the following day the defence opened and promised to clear away the suspicion that had been attached to the unfortunate prisoner.

Poor May took the stand. The excitement was intense. You could have heard a pin drop at that moment. She gives her testimony in a clear, firm voice, though she is very pale and trembling with weakness. She shows where the prisoner had passed the evening of that fatal night. Mr. Derville testifies as to the carriage which he had provided. The defence show that the greatest love existed between the prisoner and the deceased; that the prisoner, harking to the deceased's counsel, had abandoned his dissipated course.

A vast amount more testimony is adduced. The witnesses are examined and cross-examined, and at last it is over and the evidence is closed.

Then arose the senior counsel for the defence to sum up.

He began in a low but distinct voice, gradually gaining in strength, and power, and pathos, and swelling in musical cadence throughout the room.

He spoke of the love of the deceased for the innocent man who stood before them, accused of a crime as monstrous as it was improbable. As to the carriage, they had proved that it had been provided in all kindness by Mr. Derville, the prisoner's friend. Was it right that an act of kindness should be made to tell against the prisoner — an act which had been done without the knowledge of the young man? He spoke of the conversation between Derville and Frederick on the morning of the arrest, when the former, who had heard the rumors and read the article accusing the prisoner, urged him to leave the city. What had been the prisoner's answer? He wondered at the request: he was surprised. The shock that his system had received on that eventful morning had thrown him on a bed of sickness. He spoke of the suffering the young man had undergone in the solitude of his prison-cell, accused of a crime of which he knew himself to be innocent. It was bad enough for a guilty man, in his prison. What, then, must an innocent being suffer? He spoke in words so tender and pathetic as to draw tears even to the eyes of the judge. He appealed directly and strongly to the feelings. The motive that the prosecution has alleged was ridiculous — the height of absurdity. They said that the safe had been ransacked and the will taken out. How did they know a will was there? Was there, in fact, a will? They must first prove that the deceased had made such a will as alleged. They had not. Their case fell to the ground. Proof is required, not mere statements without any foundation. As to the fact of the bloody razor, it was unaccountable. The prisoner knew nothing of it. Was it likely that the murderer would hide the instrument of his guilt where it could so easily be found? It was not probable. It

7

would be a folly such as no one not naturally a fool would be guilty of.

We cannot speak as he spoke, nor use the language he used. We merely give the substance of his speech. It was not so much what he said as the manner in which he said it.

He criticised the evidence and dissected it piece by piece, and showed how weak the case against the accused was. Nothing was left untouched, and he concluded in a powerful appeal to the jury, charging them to think well and carefully before deciding; to remember the great and stern duty which rested on them; to remember that a life hung upon their decision. If the prisoner was guilty, he should, by all means, be punished; but he was not guilty; he was innocent — a victim of circumstances. There was no positive proof against him; the feeling against him had been very great and bitter, and he had been condemned by the press before he was tried at all. There were, at the least, strong doubts of his guilt, and he was entitled to a verdict as just as it would be righteous — a verdict of acquittal.

He sat down. He had made a powerful appeal for the prisoner, and after he had finished, opinions wavered again. The evidence was not so damning and conclusive as it had at first appeared.

The prisoner thanked him with his eyes.

And now the District Attorney is summing up. See, how eagerly they listen to his words! How eloquent he is! What rapt attention is paid to his powerful speech!

Oh, be very careful what you do, my friend; you know not how soon it may be brought up and made to tell terribly against you.

How he dwells upon the life the prisoner has been leading! How he dwells upon every little minute act that can possibly injure the man who stands there and listens aghast to his burning words; the man who longs to cry out, "You lie! it is a lie! a lie! it is not so!" but dares not, cannot; is bound to the rock of silence by chains which he is powerless to break; who must sit there, and listen to all that is said against him without a murmur, but can only shake his head dissentingly.

The chains which the prosecution have woven around him stagger him. He thinks he is dreaming; he hardly knows whether he is guilty or innocent. He asks himself, "Can it be?" He is in a doubt about it himself, so strong is the evidence against him. Could he have killed his father unknowingly? This doubt is agonizing! He hardly knows what he is to think. Oh, it is fearful!

But now his accuser is speaking in eloquent language of the agony and anguish of mind the dead man suffered on account of this unnatural son, who had taken what he could never return — life — from him to whom he owed his existence. He was aware that it seemed unnatural, impossible, but it was a stern reality.

He dwelt for a long time on this subject. Then he spoke on the subject of the carriage, which had been provided for the prisoner's escape. He spoke on this carriage, on this little incident, at great length.

Then, as to the motive. The prisoner knew that the deceased had made a will, which practically disinherited him. To destroy this will was a great object of the

prisoner.   He wanted money.   He must have it.
And so he murdered his father in cold blood.   For
what?   Had he not shown why?   Was not the motive
sufficient?   Was it not apparent?

And so he went on — at times pathetic, then stern
and accusing, dwelling upon everything at length,
until he had made out the guilt of the prisoner almost
conclusively.

They listened to him attentively in amazement and
with horror.   How black everything looked against
the unfortunate prisoner, who sat there with his head
bowed at last, perfectly powerless!

The speech was ended in the usual way.   He demanded justice, only justice, and then sat down amid
murmurs of applause, which were quickly hushed.

Then came the charge.   It was fair and impartial.
The judge laid down the law; then presented the evidence in a succinct, clear manner.   There was no bias
one way or another.

The effect of the charge was to set the people thinking.   It gave them time to recover from the influence
of the eloquence of the counsel.

And now the jury have retired.

Speculation is rife as to their verdict.   Will it be
guilty, or not guilty; or will they disagree?   The judge
sits listlessly in his chair.   The lawyers are very cool.
The people breathe a little.

What keeps the jury out so long?   What can they
be arguing about?   They will certainly disagree.

Oh, this terrible suspense!

They have come in for further information.

Then they retire again.

They are out a long time, surely.

But now, see — still! here they come. How solemn they look, as they take their places!

No one breathes; how suffocating the air seems! This silence is terrible. But now it is broken by the clerk of the court.

" Prisoner, stand! "

The prisoner stands.

" The jury will please rise! "

The jury rise.

" Prisoner, look on the jury! "

The prisoner does so.

" Gentlemen of the jury, have you agreed upon your verdict? "

Ah, listen!

The foreman answers :

" We have."

How still and quiet is the court-room!

" And how do you find — guilty, or not guilty? "

It is absolutely suffocating!

But, ha! Oh, God! listen to the answer!

What is it? What do they say? Oh, God! no! no! y——

" GUILTY! "

The echo replies:

" GUILTY! "

The prisoner stands firm. But deaden your ears to that terrible, unearthly shriek! Oh, it is awful! Some one has fainted. There is a slight commotion, while the prisoner staggers, and, unable longer to control his emotion, shrieks out one word in a tone of exquisite suffering and anguish :

7 *

"MAY!"

But now they have borne the lifeless form out, and quiet is restored again.

The defence request that the jury be polled.

One by one they record their verdict. They all answer :

"Guilty !"

The sentence is being pronounced, but the prisoner only hears the last words:

" —— There to be hanged by the neck until you are dead, and may God, in His infinite goodness, have mercy on your soul ! "

CHAPTER X.

THE BITTERNESS OF THE SOUL.

IT is a fine, bright day outside.   The air is full of a soft, sweet calmness that sets you thinking and dreaming, and makes you feel indolent and sleepy. You have seen such days, when the blood seems hardly to course through the veins ; when the mind wanders far away, and the eyelids have an almost irresistible tendency to close.   The soft breeze sweeps across your heated brow ; oh ! so delicious and cooling.   You do not feel like working, or getting into a passion ; the dreamy softness in the air has a soothing effect, and makes you feel at rest.   Everything appears beautiful to your sight ; and, if confined to the city, you long, oh ! so fervently, for a short sail on the river, and a glimpse of the green trees and blooming fields of the country. You feel at rest, at peace; and you do not think that there are other human beings like yourself, from whom the sunshine, the refreshing breeze, the beauties of the day are all excluded ; who are suffering untold agony; who are crying out in anguish and passion, and cursing the day that had witnessed their entrance into a world naturally good and beautiful, but made what it is by those who live in it.

Nevertheless, it is true. No sunshine, no cooling breeze steals through the dark portals of the city prison, into the cell which seems to mock at the suffering of the man so young, who paces up and down while he speaks to the woman who sits by the side of the bed.

The cell is continually reminding him, that, though he is in good health, and might live for years, he is dying, dying fast; that at a certain hour of a certain day that is approaching — it seems to him with lightning-like rapidity — his heart will cease to beat, and the warm blood will not course any more through his veins. It is a terrible thing to be placed face to face with death ; to see the ghostly visitor stretch out his skeleton hand toward you, who are powerless to move beyond his reach ; to feel his icy hand touch your body, so warm with life. Oh, it is terrible !

"It is not right; it is wrong and cruel and unjust," he was saying, in a tone that showed the agony he suffered could be felt, but never told ; " I have no rest, no peace, only darkness wherever I turn my eyes. I ask myself, is it a dream ? And then I look around. No ! The terrible reality forces itself upon my mind. I am

dying! I curse the day that gave me birth! I ask
myself why was I born to such a fate? I shall go
wild, wild, I tell you!"

"Hush; be calm, Frederick. There is no help for
it, or you would not be here. It would be better if
you could die now, for then you would escape the ignominy of the other. But, no, that must not be, for they
would say that you acknowledged your guilt by taking
your own life. And that shall never be! They shall
never say that you admitted the crime for which they
have condemned you! Be strong and firm in your
innocence, and remember, that however they may judge
you here on earth, there is a God above us all who can
see into the innermost recesses of the heart; who knows
the truth, and who is just!"

"And who is just?" he repeated, almost mockingly,
continuing in a passionate, bitter tone: "Some men
have wealth, luxury, happiness; others have only
poverty, misery, starvation! Is this right, is this just,
Mrs. Farly? Some women have every comfort a
human being can enjoy; others are compelled to sell
their very souls for a morsel of bread! Is this right, is
this just, Mary Farly? If we are all His children,
why are we not treated alike? Misery to you, and
happiness to him — is that just? Some men commit
murder and escape; others are innocent and hang. Is
that just? I tell you I am innocent, innocent, innocent as the babe unborn! And yet I am condemned
to the gallows! I am called murderer, assassin, loathed,
despised, scorned, pitied! The thought of death is
terrible to the guilty! To see day by day slip by with
ceaseless rapidity; to know that you are well, might

live for years, and yet must die; to see death coming
nearer and nearer to you every moment; to know that
at a certain hour you must walk, powerless and helpless, to certain death! Can you realize what this is?
Can you appreciate what an exquisite invention of torture this is? They say it is an easy death. It may
be. But it is the agonizing thought, which cannot be
stopped, that torments you before that day comes which
you are aware is to be your last day on earth! Ah!
It is a torture rack, an exquisite invention of cruelty!
It is terrible enough to a guilty wretch; but when one
is innocent, what must it be then? You cannot imagine
what it is to an innocent being, possessed of a sensitive
mind, to know that he is called murderer, assassin; is
loathed, despised, scorned; his life-blood craved for,
and yet is pitied by the sentimental few, who pity while
they think him guilty! Bah! And this is what
you call just! Is it? is it? is it right? is it just?
No! — ”

She had listened to him thus far in a sort of horrible
fascination, that enchained her attention, and rendered
her unable to utter a word; but now she interrupted
him:

“Stop! stop! Frederick,” she cried, with outstretched hands, “you know not what you are saying,
nor how you are paining me. You are angry, and
half-crazed, or you would never speak so! I cannot
think that in your right mind you would say what you
have said. Stop, I implore you; for your own sake,
for my sake, for the sake of her who loves you with an
unutterable love, but who is resigned; who would
rather you should die, than live to be pointed out and

F

called a murderer; who has bowed her head before
Him, and said, 'Thy will be done;' for the sake of
your angel father, and your sainted mother, who look
down on you from heaven, and know your innocence,
I beg you, I implore you, do not talk in that sacri-
legious way, but place your faith in Him!   'He moves
in a mysterious way His wonders to perform.'

> What, oh what is the wealth of the Indies,
>   Compared to the boon of a priceless love?
> What, oh what are the pleasures of earth,
>   Compared to the bliss of heaven above?"

She stopped for a moment, and then continued:
"When He commanded Abraham of old to sacrifice
the son whom he loved so well, the son of his old age,
his Isaac, upon the altar, did that great patriarch hesitate, and say, 'It is wrong, it is cruel, it is unjust?'
No! He wept, but he obeyed the will of his Almighty
Father, and led his son, his Isaac, to the sacrificial
altar! Oh, it is a grand, a great story! It teaches
us that they who place their faith and trust in Him
will never be deserted, need never fear; for He is
good, He is just!   What is earth compared to heaven?
So long as he knows your innocence, what if the world
say you are guilty?"

"But it is an ignominious death; you yourself
said so."

"Did I? I was wrong. No death is ignominious
to the innocent, only to the guilty. Place your faith
in Him, trust in Him, pray to Him to forgive your
sins. The repentant shall be forgiven, even at the
eleventh hour. He doeth all things for the best; there

is good in everything. His purpose may not be known, cannot be seen by us; but it is good. It may seem strange, cruel, unjust to us poor mortals; but it is not so. It is not for us to question, or ask why, but only to obey — to say 'Thy will, not mine, be done.' I know it seems hard, *is* hard to say, but the soul should rise superior to the body and the mind. Believe me, He doeth all things for the best. Only trust in Him and you are safe.

> I can hear him in the sunshine;
> In tempest and storm I hear
> His voice a saying unto me,
> Place all your faith and trust in me;
> Have faith and ye need not fear."

She spoke like one inspired, with such earnestness and evident sincerity, as to make him repent the words he had uttered in the bitterness of his soul.

*　　*　　*　　*　　*　　*　　*

It is the day before the execution.

Hear what the prisoner says to his devoted friend — the friend who had suffered so much, and yet whose mission it had been to conceal her own grief and console others.

"You say she is resigned. I am glad of it. I, too, am resigned. I do not fear death now. I have thought and thought and thought of it, until the idea has become familiar to my mind, and I think of it no more. Death has lost its terrors for me now — it would really be a disappointment were I to live. God is just, and whatever is is right."

*　　*　　*　　*　　*　　*　　*

[From the New York ——.]

Yesterday was a beautiful day. What a contrast to the scene which was enacted in the yard of the Tombs, where an unnatural son expiated his terrible crime!

At twelve o'clock noon, yesterday, Frederick Wyndham, the parricide, paid the penalty of the crime of which he was convicted and found guilty beyond the possibility of a doubt. The evidence was all against him; he was clearly and undoubtedly proved guilty, notwithstanding the eloquence of the able counsel who defended him.

Our readers are all familiar with the facts of the tragedy, the subsequent arrest and trial of the assassin, and yet a brief synopsis may not be uninteresting.

(Here followed the synopsis.) Yesterday the prisoner had an audience with his steadfast friends, Mr., Mrs. and Miss Derville, Mr. Smithson and his lady friend. The scene was affecting in the extreme. The parting between the unfortunate man, who still professes his innocence, notwithstanding the terrible array of facts against him, and his betrothed, brought tears even to the eyes of those who have become accustomed to such scenes.

At twelve o'clock the prisoner announced himself ready, and marched with a proud, firm step, and head erect, to the frowning gallows. There were only a few spectators present outside of the officials and reporters.

The unfortunate man allowed himself to be pinioned calmly. The Rev. Mr. —— offered up a prayer. The prisoner heard the death-warrant read in silence. When asked if he had anything to say, he replied:

"I forgive my enemies. I thank you all for the

kindness you have shown me during my prison-life. I
have made my peace with God. I am willing to die,
but I am innocent; by the Heaven above me, I swear
that I am innocent."

Then the black cap that was to shut out the sunlight
forever from his eyes, was drawn over his face.

Silence and dread seemed to hang over everything.
"No man dared to look aloft; fear was on every
soul."

The silence was broken by the sharp twang of a
rope, and the unfortunate being was jerked from his
feet into the air. There he hung between heaven and
earth.

How black and still it seemed!

Once or twice the legs were drawn up as if in pain.
That was all.

He died easy — of strangulation. At half-past
twelve the body was cut down and life pronounced
extinct. The remains were delivered to his friends
for interment.

So ended the last act of the drama; and while we
cannot but feel pity that one so young should have
come to such an untimely and ignominious end, we
hope that his fate will prove a warning to others who
are even now treading in his footsteps, and giving full
sway to unbridled and vicious passions, which, if not
controlled and kept in check, must sooner or later end
in a death of shame and ignominy.

8

CHAPTER XI.

CAPITAL PUNISHMENT.

IT was, indeed, true. Frederick Wyndham had walked with a firm, even tread, his head erect, to the scaffold.

If he shuddered inwardly as he looked on the dread instrument of death, whatever he may have felt — and who can tell the feelings of a human being at such a moment? — he showed no outward signs of emotion.

He did not meet his death with that bravado which says, "I will die like a man." They flatter themselves who say so; they do not die like men, but like dogs.

It was the knowledge that he was innocent which upheld him in this terrible hour. All the joy and pleasure that he had anticipated in his life had gone out.

We have already quoted from a morning paper, showing that he died protesting his innocence.

The evening journals had all come out with extras, and the newsboys had shouted "Extra! Full particulars of the execution!"

The papers were greedily snapped up, for there is a sort of horrible fascination in this kind of reading.

What is the argument in favor of capital punishment? What its object? The argument, and the only plausible plea in its favor, is that the interests of society require it. This argument is hypothetical and fallacious; and the best proof that it is so is the fact that where it has been abolished, and imprisonment for life substituted in its stead, the interests of society have been as well protected as they ever were.

But why, say you, should the respectable portion of the inhabitants be compelled to support for life the criminal?

If this be your argument, then, why not hang all criminals, robber, and burglar, and forger, as well as murderer? This was at one time the law in England, and yet you look back to that time with horror, pronounce such laws barbarous, and the age in which they were enacted uncivilized. And, notwithstanding, you continue to hang murderers! Is not hanging a relic of barbarism?

You reply with the Bible—an eye for an eye, a tooth for a tooth. If you take those words literally, we do not hesitate to pronounce them the law of savages,—the words of barbarism and not of humanity. To our mind, they are not meant to be taken in their literal sense, but merely as signifying the law of redress or compensation,—not the law of vengeance.

WHAT is the object of capital punishment? Vengeance? No; the law is not revengeful; the law punishes no man from motives of revenge or malice. No one will pretend that the law is vengeful. Will any one say that the law hangs a criminal merely for the purpose of taking his life? No! the law is rather inclined to be merciful.

The object of capital punishment is to prevent crime. Does it do so? If it is terrifying, it has not shown itself to be so; for, take up your paper and see how many murders you find recorded there. You say you hang a man "as a warning to others." And how many

men you have hanged as a warning to others! And
with what result? Is murder the less?

We say that you cannot prevent crime. Men in the
heat of passion do not stop to think, and law cannot
so change human nature as to prevent men getting into
a passion. Men who will commit murder in cold blood
cannot be deterred by any fear of the law. Men under
the influence of evil passions will murder other men, in
spite of all examples, while humanity remains as it is.

If, then, you hang men "as a warning to others,"
capital punishment has utterly failed of its object.
And we further say that criminals will be found to
prefer that the law should punish murder with death,
than with imprisonment for life; and for this very
simple reason, among others, it is in their favor in this,
that it gives them a loophole of escape. Juries are
averse to finding a verdict of murder in the first degree. It is useless saying to them, "Think of the dead
man," when the living man is before them. It is useless saying, "You have only to bring in the verdict;
you have nothing to do with the punishment." They
know—and how can they help knowing it?—that it is
their verdict which condemns the man to death. And
so, wherever and whenever it is possible, a jury will
shirk bringing in such a verdict. This is the reason
why so many trials have been made mere farces by the
ridiculous and utterly absurd verdicts which juries will
bring in whenever it is possible — verdicts totally un-
warranted by the facts and evidence.

"There are many questions," says a writer on this
subject, "where the accused is either guilty of murder
in the first degree, or not guilty at all. The known

bad character of the individual, the moral certainty that he committed the crime, avail nothing with many (the majority, say we) jurymen, unless something more certain than the best circumstantial evidence is furnished to convict him. They must either send him to the gallows, or set him free to prey again upon society. If the alternative were imprisonment for life, his conviction would follow, the jury feeling that he would not be robbed of any slight possibility there might exist of his proving his innocence afterward, and, at all events, society would be no longer a sufferer through him."

But, you say, if we imprison him for life, he may be pardoned soon after his conviction. To remedy and prevent this, we answer, Take away the pardoning power in such cases, unless where it is afterwards proved that the prisoner has suffered an evident injustice.

That capital punishment — that the effect of an execution, and the circumstances accompanying it — is demoralizing, cannot be denied. It has a tendency to feed the lower and baser instincts of humanity, and to deaden the finer sensibilities. And you will find by observation that an execution is immediately followed by one or more murders.

Unless the object of the law in continuing this relic of barbarism, capital punishment, is merely to kill, or, in other words, to murder with safety, then capital punishment has undoubtedly failed of its purpose; and if, as we have endeavored to show, the substitution of imprisonment for life would result in the better and surer punishment of criminals, who now frequently escape by reason of juries being possessed of human natures, and also prevent all danger of persons being

8 *

hanged on strong circumstantial evidence, who may afterwards be found to have been innocent (as in many cases in bygone years), then undoubtedly capital punishment should be abolished.

The worst use to which you can put a man, says Horace Smith, is to hang him.

Let us try imprisonment for life. If the result proves detrimental, is it not easy, if it becomes necessary, to return to the old system?

We know Frederick Wyndham to have been innocent, but it must be remembered that at the time everything was against him. There was only his own bare assertion as to his innocence. What we know, was not known then to the world.

The evidence was purely circumstantial, but it was very strong. He was generally condemned as guilty. Outside of his immediate friends, probably no one thought him innocent.

He was a victim to circumstances, and to popular excitement.

That the community thought him guilty, and believed they were doing right in ridding themselves of this unfortunate man, there can be no doubt. For the sake of humanity we must believe this.

And so he had met the death of a felon: this young man who had such a joyful, happy prospect before him so short a time previously.

He was not the only man who had been executed for a crime of which he was entirely innocent; nor is it probable, while capital punishment continues in force and men can be hanged on circumstantial evidence, he will be the last innocent being to suffer death at the hands of the law.

CHAPTER XII.

A BURGLAR.

IT is just one year to-day since Frederick Wyndham suffered the extreme penalty of the law.

May Derville and her parents had immediately after the execution departed for Europe, and are now on their way home.

Mary Farly is still with the Smithsons, but is to join the Dervilles on their return, for she has promised May to live with her.

It must be remembered that Mr. Smithson's cottage stands alone, at some distance from any other habitation. Ivy vines clamber up its walls, while immense trees extend their protecting branches almost into the windows.

It is night, and everything seems wrapped in slumber. Not a sound disturbs the silence, with the exception of the rain, which has been pouring steadily down, as if the floodgates of heaven had been opened, ever since the break of day.

But, now, look closely. See that man's form stealing slowly and carefully along.

He stops under that great tree by the side of the cottage. You can scarcely see him in the darkness.

He looks around him cautiously and warily, every sense on the alert. He listens intently, striving to catch the slightest sound. It is easy seeing that his presence here is for no good purpose. His every movement shows him to be one well acquainted with the art — if such it may be called — of burglary.

If we may believe the gleam of satisfaction in his eyes, he hears no sound except the incessant pattering of the rain as it descends from on high, drenching him to the skin. His object is plain. He is here for the purpose of theft.

Now watch him. How nimbly, how like a cat he climbs up the tree, hand over hand! His foot slips, and he feels a cold chill run through him; but he regains his equilibrium. A muttered curse escapes his lips, and he stops to listen again. He seems satisfied.

He climbs out on the limb of the tree. He must be careful; the least false move will be his death. He dares not look down below him for fear of becoming dizzy.

He extends one hand, holding fast with the other to the branch, and gently attempts to raise the window. There was no catch to it. It went up silently; but, nevertheless, he hesitated a moment before leaping into the room. But the room is unoccupied. Evidently it is a spare chamber for the use of visitors.

He is drenched to the skin, but he is in the room. Thus far all has worked to his satisfaction.

"Now for it!" he mutters in a tone of determination.

Cautiously opening the room door, he stands in the hall and peers through the darkness.

With a noiseless tread he steals along, all the while listening intently for the slightest sound. But, ha! his foot slips on something, and he stumbles. He curses his luck inwardly, and remains perfectly motionless for a few seconds.

Has any one heard him?

Yes; slight as has been the sound, Mrs. Smithson, lying awake in bed, has heard it, and is startled.

How is it that we can generally feel the presence of a thief?

She awoke her husband quietly.

"There is some one in the house," she whispered.

"Nonsense!" he answers, drowsily.

"I tell you there is; I heard him stumble. Listen!"

Sure enough, now that his suspicion is aroused, he can hear the stealthy footsteps moving along.

Quietly getting out of the bed, completely awakened, he slips on his clothes, and, armed with a revolver, noiselessly opens his room door, which the burglar has passed, and stands in the hall.

He can perceive a man's form in the darkness before him, and stealthily approaching, he creeps up behind the intruder. The latter turns almost instinctively, just as Smithson makes a spring and bears him heavily to the floor, the barrel of his revolver shining in the gloom.

There is not much of a struggle between them. The burglar, completely surprised, and already weakened from exposure and other causes, is easily overcome.

A robber, as a general thing, is a coward. He is as much afraid of you as you possibly can be of him. If he can avoid it safely, he will not do you bodily harm; for, say what he will, however bad the law, he fears it. Fear continually walks by his side. Corner him, however, and he will struggle with the desperation that is born of that very fear. A cornered rat will turn at bay. It is the same with that other species of rat — the robber. If he can possibly escape without shedding blood, he will.

It was desperation alone that enabled this burglar to struggle the little he did. He had been taken by surprise, from behind, and before he had time to recover from the shock of the sudden attack, his opponent was on top of him.

This opponent had many advantages. He was physically stronger, and, besides, he had a revolver, charged with the leaden messengers of death, which was pointed directly at the burglar's head, so that the latter could almost feel the deadly weapon pressing against his temple.

"Remain perfectly quiet — not a movement, or I fire!" whispered Smithson, quickly, in a tone there was no mistaking.

The burglar ceased to struggle, and wisely obeyed his captor's command. His life was not one to be envied, wished for, or enjoyed; but it was life, nevertheless, and it was dear, and he clung to it.

> —— It's easy saying you'd gladly die,
> When death seems far away;
> But just wait till he comes to your bedside,
> And see if you bid him stay!

By this time the servants had been aroused, and, though trembling with fright, they came, with lights, to their master's assistance.

At Smithson's command a rope was quickly brought to him, and the burglar speedily and securely bound, hand and foot.

What was to be done with him now?

They must wait for the morning; so they carried him in silence into the dining-room below.

They laid him on the floor. He did not speak; he had become sullen, moody, stolid. He only looked at them as if to say :

" Well, now you have me, what are you going to do with me ? "

It was at this moment that Mary Farly, alarmed by the unusual disturbance, entered the room.

The state of affairs was quickly explained to her.

Then her glance fell upon the burglar. His eyes were closed.

She pressed her hands to her temples and staggered violently, and would have fallen, but that Mr. Smithson caught her in his arms.

Did she recognize the captive ?

" What is the matter, Mary ? " whispered Mr. Smithson.

" It is nothing — nothing ; only a sudden faintness," she answered, with a painful smile.

But they could not help noticing her agitation, and wondering at it.

The burglar opened his eyes and gazed full at her. If she recognized him, evidently he did not her. All his look said was, " Well, who are you ? "

But that look satisfied her, and set all doubts at rest ; and, whispering to Smithson, she left the room hurriedly.

He followed her. She stood in the hall near the stairway.

" What are you going to do with him ? " she said, hoarsely, pointing to the room.

"I don't know," he answered. "We will have to keep him until the morning, and then deliver him up to the authorities for trial."

"For trial?"

There was something in her voice, as she repeated the words, that made him look at her. She was deathly pale, and trembling, as if with an ague.

"No! no! You must not — you must not — shall not!"

"Shall not?" he echoed in surprise.

"No; for my sake. Oh, Mr. Smithson, bend low your head! He is — he is —" the remaining words were whispered very faintly.

He had but time to raise his head when she lifted her hand mechanically and fell swooning into his arms.

CHAPTER XIII.

THE END OF A SAD LIFE.

IT may be that in the lives of all of us there shall be a day, to record the events of which would take many pages of manuscript, while the balance of our days could, as a distinguished lady novelist puts it, be summed up in the simple phrase:

"This man or this woman continued to exist."

Therefore, as we are writing a life romance, we hope the reader will not be surprised at rapid changes and events, nor at the lapse of time between the various scenes, to which we devote but a few words.

It would be folly to describe every day, when it is only a few of them that require our attention, so far as this story is concerned.

It is some three weeks since the events recorded in the preceding chapter occurred.

Whatever may have been the reason, the burglar had not been delivered up to the tender mercies of the law, for here he is, thin, pale, and emaciated, with the seal of death resting on his face, under clean, white coverlets, with Mary Farly for his nurse.

Chilled and wet to the skin on that night when he entered the Smithsons' cottage, it was no wonder that when the morning broke, the burglar lay helpless in the agonies of fever and delirium.

They carried him up to a spare room, and placed him in the bed, and then sent for a disciple of Esculapius.

The worthy doctor examined his patient, and shook his head gravely. It was a bad case; and on this morning he had taken Mr. Smithson aside, and said to him:

"There is no use in my coming again. There is no hope; he cannot live. His constitution is completely shattered and ruined, and he is a mere wreck. I can do nothing more for him. He does not suffer much bodily pain, but he cannot live more than a few days —two or three at the utmost. Let me know when he is dead, and I will give you a certificate."

Smithson repeated the doctor's words to Mary Farly very gently and tenderly.

He had expected her to be surprised and pained; but she listened to him very calmly. All she said was:

9   G

"It is better for him and for me."   •

She is sitting by the window looking out upon the bright day and the cloudless sky. Her day was once bright, her sky once as cloudless as the sky she was gazing on. And now, what a change, what a change the last few years of her life had wrought!

In the happy days of her childhood, those happiest days of life to look back upon, when the world seemed bright and fair to her inexperienced eyes, and misery was a word unknown to her, could she have dreamed that she would come to this!

Ah! life is a mystery, and death is its solution — the dream of life, and the awakening of death — and looking forward into the shadowy, unknown future, which a wise Providence has veiled from our eyes, who can say what changes time may make?

Mark well the present, and seek not to penetrate the mysteries of the future. The past is dead, the future not yet born, but the present is before us — *here*. Our lives are to a great extent what we make them; as ye sow, so shall ye reap.

Mary Farly could not refrain from turning her eyes upon the invalid, whose days were numbered, and whose life-tide was ebbing fast, even as he lay there apparently dozing, as she thought of those days which had passed away forever.

Presently she arose and began walking — or, rather, pacing — with an almost noiseless tread, up and down the room, in the manner of one whose mind is disturbed, and so, unconsciously, her thoughts found vent in words:

"And it has come to this!" she said, half aloud.

"It has come to this, that all my dreams of happiness have faded — were but dreams — and that life which I had pictured to myself as beautiful and noble, a Utopia of my imagination; that I am doomed to bring only misery to them who are so unfortunate as ever to love me, and my life not only to be a curse to myself, but also to others. Leslie Wyndham loved me; he was murdered, and his son hanged. And see him, my husband — husband still, despite all the suffering he has caused me, for whom I rejected a noble love, and to whom I have ever been true — dying a thief, a common thief! Why was I ever born? What have I done to deserve this punishment?"

But, see, look at the invalid leaning on his elbow, his face full of agony, and his sunken eyes staring and gazing at the woman who still continues her restless pacing up and down the room; those eyes which burn like coals of fire, so full of memories of the past, as they conjure themselves up in an instant; those eyes so full of recognition.

He has heard every word she has uttered. They have imprinted themselves indelibly on his brain, and they almost set him wild.

He utters a hardly distinct groan. She turns to him, and as he falls back upon the pillow, one word, full of the most poignant anguish and self-reproach, escapes his lips:

"MARY!"

She looks on his pallid face and reads the truth there.

It has come — that which she has expected, has

known must have come sooner or later. If he had not guessed it, she would have told him ere death claimed him as his own; for she had felt it to be her duty to disclose the truth — the secret which had been preying on her mind, and, in a few short weeks, made her appear agêd.

Ever since that night when she had recognized in the burglar, though he did not recognize her, the man who was bound to her by the holiest of ties, the man whom she had sworn at the altar to love, honor, cherish, and obey — her husband — Mary Farly had undergone in the solitude of her chamber an agony which few people can appreciate, or are doomed to suffer.

She had asked herself time and time again, if she had treated this man as she should have; if she had done her whole duty towards him, had acted rightly, and for the best. She could not imagine how this man, who had been born in the midst of luxury and wealth, who had been tenderly reared, cultivated and educated, who before his marriage had never known the miseries of poverty, or aught of suffering; whose mind had been trained in the pathway of truth, honor, and principle, but whose jealous disposition had been his curse, could ever have fallen so low, could ever have descended to the degradation of a common thief, without honor, without principle, an enemy to others and to himself; how he who had known a mother's love, a mother's tender care and solicitude, and all the comforts and pleasure that wealth could furnish, or the mind desire, could ever have fallen so low as to become a disgrace to her who bore him. Ah! could that mother have foreseen that the son she idolized would come to this!

Mary Farly did not know the worst yet — the terrible truth she was soon to learn; but she asked herself if she was not to blame, partly, for this man's downfall. Had she not been in fault?

Had she done right in continuing on her terms of intimacy with Leslie Wyndham against her husband's express wishes and commands, thus encouraging and feeding his jealousy? She knew his disposition; and now, when it was too late, she looked back and asked herself would it not have been better, and would she not have been spared all the trouble and misery she had known, had she obeyed his wishes for the time, and by mild persuasion and gentle words, and all those little arts which women know so well, have gradually soothed his jealousy, until at length it wore off altogether. Would it have worn off? Would he ever have been freed from it? That was not the question; but had she acted wisely, and done her whole duty? Had she done right in leaving him? Had she done her best? had she tried her greatest to reclaim him from the downward course into which his footsteps had strayed? Was she blameless?

Ah! it was too late now. The time when she might have been able to have reclaimed him had passed away forever. She could repent the folly of those days now, but she could not call them back.

"Let him who is without sin among you cast the first stone." We can never tell how we would act, until placed in a position for acting. It is folly to say we would do so and so in such and such a case; only when we are placed in the position can we know what we will do.

9 *

And now the long separated husband and wife stood
face to face. What a lifetime they passed in that one
moment after he had said,

"Mary!"

"You have recognized me at last," she said, trem-
blingly. "Oh, James, I knew you the very moment
my eyes fell on your face."

"And that is the reason why I was not given up to
the police," he murmured. "I see it now."

And then, in an eager, repentant voice, that went
straight to her heart, and his sunken eyes lit up with
all the old love and tenderness, he cried:

"Oh, Mary! Mary! can you forgive the past?"

"It is for me to ask your forgiveness, James," she
answered, in a voice fraught with emotion. "I have
suffered — oh! so much — from the thought that I have
not treated you rightly. I should have broken off my
friendship with Leslie Wyndham when you told me
to. But, oh, James, you did not know him. He was
honest, good, pure, noble."

A change came over him as she spoke of the
murdered man. He shuddered, and then said, bitterly:

"Why have you spared me? Why did you ever
care for me? Why have you saved me from the
police? I forgot that you are not my wife. I forgot
that you were divorced from me and married to him!"

"Who told you that?" she cried. "It is a lie!
He loved me, he aided me, he would have married me,
had I been divorced; but I remained as I was — your
wife!"

He had half arose in the bed as she spoke, his sunken

eyes seeming as though they would start from their sockets, and his features convulsed with unspeakable agony.

He grasped her arm almost savagely, as she concluded, and said, hoarsely:

"No, no! it cannot be! Say it is not so, Mary! For God's sake, say it is not so!"

His vehemence, the tortured expression on his face, startled and mystified her; and for a moment she was silent. Then she answered solemnly:

"It is the truth, James; I swear it is the truth. He was only my friend. You are dying, James, and I forgive all the suffering you have caused me."

But his hand relaxed the savage grasp of her arm, and he fell back, covering his face with both hands, crying in agony:

"Good God! Only her friend! What have I done! Oh, God! what have I done! Mary, Mary! God help me! *I murdered him!*"

The truth flashed across her mind in an instant. That which, when reading in a novel, she had deemed utterly impossible, was not a fiction, but was a truth.

She started with horror. She could only utter one word with white, blanched lips, while he moaned and tossed about the bed in the most excruciating torture:

"YOU!"

"Oh, Mary! Mary! forgive me! You shrink from me with fear! Don't — don't look at me so! Have mercy! have mercy! It is terrible! oh, it is terrible! You tremble with horror! Your husband is a murderer! Oh, Mary! Mary! do not judge me too hastily, too harshly. Listen to me; hear the whole truth. Oh, Mary! I thought you were divorced from me and married to him! I thought he had wronged me, and I was mad, mad! Have mercy! have mercy!"

And then he made a terrible confession that froze the blood in her veins as she stood before him, rigid, motionless, as if carved out of stone.

When he had finished, she could have cursed him. But, ah, even as the words are on her lips, the angels of Love and Charity whisper in her ears, and beg her not to speak them. They whisper to her to be calm; they tell her what she must do; they say, "Forgive, as you would be forgiven."

And he is tossing wildly about in his agony, and praying for her pardon.

"Oh, Mary! Mary! forgive me! I am dying, and I was mad! mad! Mercy! have mercy!"

Yes, he is dying, and she remembers the temptations that have assailed him. Shall she withhold her pardon from him now? Shall she judge him when soon he will stand before the throne of Him who alone can rightfully judge?

"The tempter is worse than the tempted," she says, solemnly. "But it was murder — it was murder — would have been murder, even if he had wronged you in the most cruel way one can wrong another. You had no right to take his life. If he had done wrong, your doing wrong could not make that right. Murder is murder, and only He alone who gave life has a right to take it. No man has a right to take the prerogative of God in his own hands, or to take the life which he cannot return."

*   *   *   *   *   *   *

She has called Mr. Smithson up. She has told him all calmly, and of her intentions for the future.

James Farly's confession has been written out. The pen is placed in his hand for signature, and he scrawls his name with trembling fingers at the bottom of the page. They sign as witnesses.

It is done; and Mary Farly holds in her hand the secret of Leslie Wyndham's murder, and the proof of the innocence of his son. .

" You forgive me, Mary, you forgive me ? " he cries, wildly. " I loved you, oh, I loved you ! "

" You have sinned, sinned deeply. I, too, have done wrong. I cannot judge you. If it will lighten your sorrow, know that I forgive you. I have a duty before me. I must clear Frederick Wyndhan's name of the obloquy which we have helped cast upon it. We are both to blame, and I hope God will forgive you as I do. Pray to Him, pray to Him, in the few short hours that remain to you."

*　　　*　　　*　　　*　　　*　　　*　　　*

She was sitting by the bedside watching him, when she observed the change that was taking place. The pallor of death was slowly creeping over his face. He lay silently and quietly, holding her hand in his. She felt his hand growing colder and colder. The old love welled up in her heart as she gazed on the wreck of the man she had known in happier days. The words of the immortal bard came to her mind :

> The evil that men do lives after them ;
> The good is oft interred with their bones.

She had known suffering and agony, but what torture must he have undergone ! Who can say ?

Whatever of suffering this man had caused her, she had known him when he was in the pride of manhood and happiness; and in that solemn moment, in the presence of the mighty bridegroom, Death, she forgave him all.

He opened his eyes suddenly, and looked at her. She stooped to hear what he might say. He essayed to speak, but could not. She heard the death-rattle in his throat; he shuddered, and then she felt the hand that held hers slowly relax its hold. She kissed him once, while her heart seemed as if it was breaking; a smile of ineffable happiness passed over his face as their lips met for the last time; something like a sigh escaped him, and then he was dead.

He, whose life had been embittered and wrecked on the shoals of passion, died quietly, with a happy smile on his face, as though he was passing into a delightful dream.

CHAPTER XIV.

JAMES FARLY'S CONFESSION.

WE must reiterate that this is not a sensational story, unless the truth can be said to be sensational.

We prefer to give James Farly's confession in our own words. As he told it, the reader may easily imagine that it was frequently interlarded by pitiful cries and laments, and many words of poignant self-reproach.

We go back to that eventful night when James Farly arrived at his wretched home, to find that his wife had, at last, deserted him.

For some days after, he remained perfectly sober. There was a sense of utter desolation about him. He could not conceal the fact from himself that he was to blame; that he had himself to thank for what he now suffered.

It is said that it is very easy to make ourselves believe that which we are anxious and desirous to believe. So it is, but not immediately. When a man first discovers himself to be in the wrong, he feels it, and no amount of self-reasoning and conscience-bribing can for some time afterwards make him feel satisfied that he is or has been wholly right.

The first few days which followed that night were spent by James Farly in ceaseless and constant brooding.

The mind, sooner or later, is sure to become in a manner more or less affected by the constant nursing of one idea. This was the case with James Farly. We have seen that, to use a mild phrase, he had always disliked Leslie Wyndham. It did not take him long to associate the cause of his wife's desertion with the latter. He came to look on him as the cause of all his troubles. The natural consequence was that in a short time he had convinced himself that he was not at all to blame, and that he owed all that had come to pass to the man who, in his language, "had come between him and his wife."

The future depended entirely now upon his advisers. The reader has already obtained an insight into the

character and nature of this man, and has seen how
weak-minded he was, and how liable, in consequence,
to be controlled by others.

This man, who had once known luxury and wealth,
soon became a beggarly outcast.   The very people who
had praised and flattered him in his days of affluence
now passed him by without a glance of recognition.
The very men who had fed upon his generosity, even
his low associates, and the dealers in alcoholic poison, refused to extend him a helping hand.   He was
shunned like some loathsome viper, and the craving
appetite for drink once more came over him.   Every
cent that he managed to earn by doing odd work went
into the till of some dram-shop.

Wandering, one day, into one of the lowest groggeries that abound in the not over-aristocratic purlieus
of Water Street, he was accosted by a man who, although
he will figure to a great extent in the events which are
to follow, it is as impossible for us to say who he really
was, as it would have been for any one who knew him
to have told.

He was one of those mysterious personages we sometimes meet, who, by some occult influence, manage to
gain access to the highest as well as to the lowest
circles of society.

This man had made the acquaintance of James Farly
long before the time of which we are writing, and with
that peculiar gift which some people have, had not
only read his character at a glance, but gained a powerful influence over him.

Now, nobody had ever seen Mr. Charles Williams,
as he called himself at this time, in a state of intoxica-

tion. He could be the gentleman among gentlemen, and *per contra.* Everybody appeared to know him, though to many, for various peculiar reasons that they would not have cared to have made public, his acquaintance was anything but desirable or advantageous.

Almost unconsciously to himself James Farly had told Mr. Charles Williams his entire history. Mr. Charles Williams had condoled with him, said he knew Leslie Wyndham, and had assisted James Farly in his downward career.

It may readily be imagined that Mr. Williams was not acting without a motive. He did know Leslie Wyndham, or rather had known him, when he was not passing under the name of Charles Williams. Leslie Wyndham had come between him and an intended victim; had spoilt and foiled one of his long-cherished "little games" just when he had imagined victory certain, and Mr. Williams had not forgotten it, though many years had intervened since then.

He was a man who boasted that he never forgot a favor nor forgave an injury; a dangerous man, who could wait for years and years, nourishing his hatred, but never forgetting or forgiving; a man who could smile and laugh with you while murder was at his heart. But he was a cool, cold-blooded, calculating, prudential villain. Your ignorant, uncultured, savage outlaw is not to be feared by the side of your educated, heartless, plotting villain. The latter by his knowledge and the main force of his mind can control a horde of uneducated, depraved brutes.

While Mr. Williams, therefore, might have liked nothing better than to have killed you, he could at the

10

same time appear on the most friendly terms with you, for he was too prudent by far to run any risk that might place his precious self in danger.

We are looking now, it must be remembered, at the inside of this man's character, and not at the side he presented to the gaze of the world. We desire to give a good insight into his character, in order that you may not be surprised at the events to follow; and we desire it also to be remembered that what is here told in a few words and in a few minutes was the work of years, done slowly, step by step, and began by hints which gradually shaped themselves into open words.

Mr. Williams, to continue, was an utterly unprincipled man, with no thoughts of a future life, little reverence for the Bible or the Creator; no thoughts that were not for and of self; no feeling for any one but himself. He had but one God, knew but one power — money. For that, could he have done so without danger to himself, he would have waded through blood. He was not afraid of hanging, but he did not care for imprisonment. Hanging was soon over; but why hang? said he, philosophically.

He was a gambler and a cheat. He moved, in his dual character, among the upper ten, and the lower ten thousand; played gentleman, gallant, aristocrat; gambler, villain, outcast, just as the occasion demanded.

And now to resume. James Farly had just been refused the poison which his appetite craved, when Mr. Williams entered the drinking den.

Williams was perfectly aware of all that had happened to Farly; but it suited him best at that time to be ignorant.

"Ah! Farly, you here?" he exclaimed, taking him by the hand, much to Farly's surprise not only at seeing, but at being recognized by him. "Hello! What's happened, old fellow? You look seedy — played out. Come! this won't do. You should have called on me; you know I am your friend. Come along and let me know what's up now. James Farly begging for a drink! and where they only sell slops! and I alive! Come along, I'll give you some of the genuine Simon Pure."

Farly was only too glad to find a friend; some one who had known him in better days, and now grasped him by the hand against which all men's hands seemed to be turned. He had not expected Williams to recognize him at all; but it was not a dream. There was one human being, at least, who still called him a friend, and so he did not offer any remonstrances when Williams took him by the hand and led him out of the vile hole.

Williams insisted on his right and privilege, as James Farly's friend, to take care of and share his home with him. And so he took him in charge.

Of course, that very evening the deserted husband told his benefactor all that had happened. Williams was not surprised; he had expected such an ending. He hastened to agree with Farly that Leslie Wyndham was, to use his own words, "at the bottom of it." He did everything in his power to inflame the passions and the hatred of Farly against the journalist.

"We" (of course, whoever injured Farly injured Williams) "have a score to settle with him some day. We can wait; that will make the interest on the debt accumulate. It is very simple to me — excuse me for talking plainly, old fellow — she has left you to join him. He will procure her a divorce somewhere, and then marry her."

In this way the days passed by. Williams inducted Farly into the mysteries of gambling, an art in which he was *au fait*, always taking care to keep him in liquor, and strengthen his hatred for Leslie Wyndham.

Gradually, and by degrees, the master villain unfolded the plan his plotting brain had conceived, to his yielding tool. It was a plan worthy of the man, and at any other time would have made James Farly recoil with horror, so deep and cold-blooded was it.

In substance, to make the story short, and expose it in all its fiendishness, it was simply this:

Mary Farly, being the wife of Leslie Wyndham, and in that case his only living near relation, with the exception of his son Frederick, in the event of his death would inherit a great portion of all he possessed, especially if his son was also "removed." The plan was to murder Leslie Wyndham, to speak plainly — Mr. Williams used a much milder word — which he (Williams) would arrange so that no suspicion should or could attach either to Farly or himself. This being done, he contracted to throw suspicion upon Frederick, and to cause his arrest and execution, the principal object in doing this being to prevent the young man from "causing us" (*i. e.*, Williams and Farly) "any trouble." Mary Farly would then come forward, of course, and put in her claim to the estate. Then it would be very easy to have the divorce set aside as fraudulent, and Farly, by this means, would not only accomplish his revenge, but also would obtain something more tangible.

All this was to be in consideration of Farly's signing a paper agreeing to give to Williams one-half of what he would acquire, upon its completion, through his wife.*

Williams did not fear that Farly would not carry out his part of the contract; he was too well aware of his power over his weak-minded tool to fear that.

This is the simple, unvarnished, bare synopsis of the plain details of this devilish plot, however abhorrent and incredible it may appear.

But it was necessary to find out first whether a divorce had been procured or not. If it had, then Mr. Williams felt perfectly sure that Leslie Wyndham and Mary Farly had consummated a marriage.

No divorce had been obtained in New York; but Williams did not imagine for a moment that it had. He knew how much easier it was to obtain such a thing in other States. In which, if any, had a divorce been procured? In order to ascertain this, both time and money would be requisite. So far as time was concerned, there was no difficulty; but it would, in all probability, require more capital than either of them possessed or might possess for months. The crafty

---

* It may seem rather strange that a man like Williams should have been so ignorant of the law on the subjects upon which the ultimate success of his plot depended, and that he should have remained so, instead of informing himself what the law on those points really was, as he could easily have done; nor can we account for this, except on the supposition that his principal and moving motive was to satisfy the hatred he felt for Leslie Wyndham on account of the matters hereinbefore mentioned, and the pecuniary object merely auxiliary. — AUTHOR.

brain was not found wanting here, though.   The capital
must be immediately acquired, and by robbery.

Mr. Williams selected a victim whom he knew
always kept a large sum of money locked up in a safe
at his house, and they agreed that in case of the detection, by any mischance, of either of them, he would remain silent in regard to the other.

This robbery was effected.   Williams secured the
plunder, but Farly fell into the hands of the police.
He kept his agreement with Williams, and remained
silent.   But, though ably defended, his trial resulted,
despite Mr. Williams' influence, in a conviction, and
sentence to five years' imprisonment.

Williams kept in constant communication with his
victim, telling him to keep up bravely in view of the
ends to be acquired, and that he had made a reserve
fund of the plunder they had obtained, and was waiting patiently until he (Farly) was released.   They
could afford to wait, he said, and let the interest accumulate.

At the expiration of his sentence, Farly was liberated.
Williams was the first person to greet him.

These years, passed in prison, and in contact with
depraved associates and hardened characters, did not
do much to improve James Farly.   This was another
debt to be settled with Leslie Wyndham.

He came out of the prison — not reformed.   If
prisons were made for purposes of reformation, they
utterly failed of their object with James Farly.   He
came out hardened, depraved, more bloodthirsty and
hating, his better nature seemingly totally warped and
dead.   He did not blame Williams as the cause of his

last degradation, but rather looked up to him, if that was possible, more than ever. The weaker mind was completely in the power and under the control of the stronger.

The search for the divorce, which had been deferred so long through his imprisonment, was immediately begun. He was very impatient, and could not brook delay. So they set out on their search and travels within a week after his liberation.

They journeyed from one place to another, choosing first the cities where Williams thought it most likely the divorce, if there was one, had been procured. It was slow, weary work, besides being expensive. Their exchequer was fast becoming exhausted, and, as yet, their trouble had all been in vain.

This consumed some time. They stopped, and gambled with varying luck, at several places. But at last they found it. Their journey was at an end; their untiring search was rewarded. There it was, the positive proof of Mr. Williams' conjectures. The date, the year — everything agreed.

"*Mary Farly* vs. *James Farly. Divorce granted.*" Thus spoke the record.

To New York again. They arrive, James Farly brooding and nursing constantly that one idea — revenge. Revenge on the man who had robbed him of his wife, and made him what he was. Oh! what a glorious revenge his would be! The words of the poet did not recur to him:

> Revenge is sweet — is sweet;
> But it is a sweet poison!

It was at this time that the haunted house opposite

Leslie Wyndham's was taken by the two men, Philip
Marton and Thomas Castle, otherwise Charles Williams
and James Farly.

If the conversation in that house between them,
which has heretofore been recorded, was unintelligible
to our readers, they will understand it now.

Suspicion points strongly to Williams having had
an accomplice in Leslie Wyndham's house. Perhaps
this accomplice did not know his principal's object.
However that may be, it is certain, that by some means,
he possessed himself of the razor, which was afterwards
such a terrible piece of evidence against Frederick
Wyndham, and gained admittance to the house on the
night he had selected for the carrying out of his plot.

They were secreted in the house when Frederick came
in. After this they allowed a couple of hours to pass,
until all became silent again. Then, removing their
shoes, stealthily, in stocking feet, they entered their
victim's sanctum. They could hear his hard breathing.

James Farly, mad with the thought of his vengeance,
now so near at hand, passed into the room where Leslie
Wyndham was sleeping, clutching a heavy revolver by
the barrel, and gazed with a fiendish joy upon the unconscious sleeper's countenance. Not a spark of pity
moved him. There lay the object of his long pent-up
hatred; there lay the man who had caused him all his
suffering — the man who, he had persuaded himself,
had wronged him in the worst possible manner one
human being can wrong another.

It was at this moment that Leslie Wyndham opened
his eyes. They fell upon the demoniac face of the man
standing by his bedside.

He recognized him instantly. Surprise, for the moment, deprived him of all power to follow his first impulse, and cry out. The next instant James Farly, with a muttered curse, was on him, one hand clutching him with a grip of iron by the throat, and strangling him.

Never for a moment, in the terrible struggle which ensued, did the maddened man loosen his grasp of his victim's throat.

The doomed man struggled desperately ; but not a word could escape his lips. In his own house, at the dead of night, he was being murdered, and could not call for assistance.

This terrible battle for life was fought in silence. James Farly dealt his victim blow upon blow with the butt end of the revolver, and with all the desperation of a maniac.

Williams sprang to his aid just in time. His hand was relaxing its grasp of Leslie Wyndham's throat. But the cry that arose to the lips of the poor victim was stifled by a heavy, terrible blow on the forehead from the revolver Williams carried. Stunned and unconscious, but not yet quite dead, he lay completely in his assassins' power.

James Farly would have stabbed him over and over in his blind fury, had not the more prudent villain withheld him, and bidding him not to let the blood spurt on his clothes, handed him Frederick's razor.

The madman quickly and with all his strength drew it across Leslie Wyndham's throat, severing it from ear to ear.

Then, when the bloody deed was accomplished, they

inflicted stab after stab on the poor body, being careful not to get any bloodstains on themselves. This was done for the purpose of making it appear that the assassin's clothes must, necessarily, have become stained with blood, and that it did so, was sufficient proof of Mr. Williams' sagacity — a quality he greatly prided himself upon. It was his boast that he always "covered his footsteps."

Mr. Williams turned his attention, when all again was silent, to the safe. He easily found the key in the murdered man's coat-pocket.

The safe was open! Before him was the object of his worship, gold; yet he did not touch it. No! He commenced ransacking and tossing the papers about, to give the impression that the assassin's object was to secure a particular paper, and not robbery. How well he succeeded we know.

At last he came across the document he had hoped to find. It was endorsed, "Last will and testament of Leslie Wyndham."

His success was, so far, all that he could have desired. He thrust the will into his capacious coat-pocket, and having seen everything placed in the position in which he wished them to be found, and followed by James Farly, who had, during the whole time his confederate was operating at the safe, remained gazing with a savage smile on the face, gashed and mutilated, of the man whom he had murdered, constantly murmuring, "Revenged! revenged!" left the house in the same silence and secrecy in which they had entered it.

What followed has been heretofore detailed.

In the immediate excitement, Mr. Williams managed, by the same covert means which had enabled
him to obtain it, to secrete Frederick Wyndham's
razor in the place where it was afterwards found.

Before proceeding further to carry out his scheme,
Mr. Williams had the prudence to allow some days to
elapse.

Of course, no suspicion entered any one's mind
when Philip Marton said he "would like to have the
villain who did it, that he might torture him to death
by inches."

Why should any one suspect the rich, elegant
Mr. Marton? But it was Mr. Marton who industri-
ously circulated the hints in regard to Frederick
Wyndham, who started never-sleeping suspicion, and
who caused the articles we have quoted from to be in-
serted and circulated by the press.

As we know, everything worked to his entire satisfaction, and James Farly (otherwise Thomas Castle),
now returned to his old state of continual intoxication,
gazed on the master villain with a feeling akin to, if
not exactly awe.

But when time passed, and Mary Farly did not
come forward to lay claim to the murdered man's
estate, Mr. Philip Marton grew uneasy, and when a
still further time elapsed and the public administrator
took charge of the effects, he became more and more
uneasy.

Suddenly a new thought struck him. In the excitement of the moment he had forgotten to make any
inquiries as to the Mary Farly who had procured a
divorce, and now it flashed across his mind that it

might, after all, have been a simple coincidence. Determined to find out and satisfy himself at once, he took a trip, keeping Farly in ignorance of his object, to the city where he had found the record. It proved, of course, as he had feared. All his trouble and plotting had been wasted and in vain. But there was no use in repining or cursing his luck, and he immediately returned to New York. He said nothing whatever on the subject, but immediately proceeded to rid himself of his blind follower.

Left alone again, and completely in the other's power, James Farly rapidly sank to the level from which Mr. Williams had taken him. He dared not think, but drowned brain and memory in the alcoholic poison.

It was in this state of degradation and abject poverty that he planned the robbery of Smithson's cottage, which, as has been seen, resulted in his detection.*

---

* In closing this chapter, we desire to say that we are fully aware of the inconsistency between the "cool, calculating, prudential villain" we have said Mr. Williams was, and his character as viewed solely in the light of the part he enacted in the murder of Leslie Wyndham. His whole plot was founded on suppositions which, however, after the finding of the record of divorce between Mary Farly and James Farly, had, with him, as much weight as truths; his ideas of the law were incorrect, and his manner of proceeding rather strange. But is there any accounting for the inconsistencies of human nature, and do we not often find the wisest men making the most simple errors?

The only way in which we can account for Williams falling into these errors is, as we have before stated, on the ground that his principal and moving motive was to satisfy the hatred he felt for his victim, and that the pecuniary motive, strong as that was with him, was merely auxiliary. This is the only explanation we can give, and if the reader thinks it worse than none at all, and wonders why we

CHAPTER XV.

SELF AND DUTY.

SUCH, in short, was the substance of the terrible confession which James Farly made with his dying breath and signed with his last strength, in the presence of the woman who was his wife and the friend whom his victim had provided for her. Such was the paper which Mary Farly carried in the bosom of her dress, and which proved the innocence of the law's victim — the victim of popular excitement — poor, ill-fated Frederick Wyndham.

What a great task this confession imposed upon Mary Farly! It rested on her to prove the innocence of Frederick Wyndham, and to rescue his name from the obloquy which was now attached to it.

The long and terrible struggle between self and duty carried on in her breast in the silence of the long night which followed James Farly's decease, left an impression that only death eradicated.

Self asked her why she should trouble herself further? The dead could not be recalled to life.

could not have constructed this story so as to have prevented our feeling any necessity for this note, we can only reiterate that ours is a matter-of-fact romance, and that all the events narrated in this chapter have actually occurred and passed into history, and that the only deviation from the facts which we have made has been to change the names of the parties, and the fate, or, rather, the lives of the murderers after accomplishing their crime.

In the case in which the facts here related came to light, they were both tried, found guilty, and executed. —AUTHOR.

11

Why inflict suffering on herself? Why not let the whole thing rest where it was, to be buried in oblivion, and let the dead past bury its dead? Duty, in its stern, unwavering voice, whispered, "Spare not thyself! You have been an innocent cause of their death. On you rests the responsibility of clearing the mystery, whatever of suffering it may entail on you, whatever sacrifices you may be compelled to make. They who conceal a crime are as bad as they who commit it. Will you regard yourself, or will you think of the dead, and the duty you owe to God to see that insomuch as lies in your power justice is done?"

If she regards the voice of duty, she must find Philip Marton, and compel him to verify James Farly's confession; for otherwise it was not and could not be complete. It would be merely regarded as the ravings of a madman or as a sensational story. But to find Philip Marton — what a hopeless task this seemed! She must find a man she had never, to her knowledge, seen, and of whom she had not the slightest description. Even his name, like a kaleidoscope, was constantly changing. And this man, too, was no ordinary person.

Self cried again and pleaded strongly. Duty, uncompromising and immovable, repeated, "Spare not thyself!"

Oh, what agony, what misery, what torture she suffered that night! Years passed in minutes. But, with the help of Him who ruleth, self was flung aside, and duty conquered.

Will she find Philip Marton?

CHAPTER XVI.

"DUST THOU ART, TO DUST RETURNETH."

THE hot summer's day is drawing to a close. Slowly the great Sun, gleaming like a ball of fire, is setting in the distant west, tinging the horizon with a reddish golden hue; the pale Queen of Night can be faintly seen gazing at her king whose reign is ending. The air is redolent of a soft, rich sweetness; the perfume of the tuberose is borne on the cool, refreshing breeze that ever and anon rustles the leaves of the majestic oak, and sways the slender branches of the mourning weeping willows. No sound disturbs the quiet; everything is still and silent as they who rest calmly here sleeping the never-ending sleep, for this is a city of the dead. Here and there the rays of the setting sun fall on a cold white monument of marble which marks the resting-place of somebody's dead. "Sacred to the memory of ——," we read, and know that some poor mortal has passed before the judgment-seat of his Maker.

What was his life? Was he happy, or was it his happiest moment when they brought him here and covered him with the mother earth from which he had sprung?

After all, what a frail tenement we live in! what a short lease we hold!

We are born, we laugh, we weep,
We love, we droop, we die.

What are our thoughts as we gaze on this home of the dead? Here is a proud, tall monument; there, only a small mound with a number written on a piece of wood thrust into the earth, tells who sleeps beneath to them he has left behind to mourn him. Even in this sacred place the pomp of wealth rears its head.

What are we thinking of? This is no place for earthly thoughts; angels are guarding this spot. Thoughts of death and the mystery which must forever remain unsolved, the mystery of the Hereafter, are uppermost in the mind now.

> We look upon the heavens,
>   And they are clear and blue,
> And in the liquid ether the eye
>   Of God shines through.

All earthly things are forgotten in the presence of the kingdom of Death; these are holy images that flit before us now.

How quiet all is! We are breathing a holier, purer atmosphere here; for this short time let us think of God. Soon we must go back and commingle with the world; here let us rest and think.

> To this complexion we must come at last.

Poor, proud mortals! What are ye in the presence of Death? What are ye that ye should dare dispute His words?

Oh! come with me here; let us not disturb the silence. We are out of the world now: this is a better place; this spot is holy ground; angels hover over it; God is here.

No more; they who sleep here have done forever with care, suffering, passion. The world is naught to them; it cannot injure, it cannot help them. They have parted with life and trouble; no care, no grief, no sorrow, can reach them now. He who sleeps beneath this grand monument is no better than he who rests beneath this simple mound; they are equal. Poor and rich stand alike in the presence of God; all are His children, for His is the kingdom of heaven, and He is Love.

Are we thinking of those exquisite lines of the poet's inspired pen?

The breezy call of incense-breathing morn,
    The swallow, twittering from the straw-built shed,
The cock's shrill clarion, or the echoing horn,
    No more shall rouse them from their lowly bed.
*   *   *   *   *   *   *

The boast of heraldry, the pomp of power,
    And all that beauty, all that wealth e'er gave,
Alike await th' inevitable hour.
    The paths of glory lead but to the grave.
*   *   *   *   *   *   *

Can storied urn, or animated bust,
    Back to its mansion call the fleeting breath?
Can honor's voice provoke the silent dust,
    Or flattery soothe the dull, cold ear of death?

No further seek his merits to disclose,
    Or draw his frailties from their dread abode,
(There they alike in trembling hope repose,)
    The bosom of his Father and his God.

How grandly beautiful the poem is! We can close our eyes and see the picture so faithfully described before us.

We can see God in everything; but it is the grave-
11 *

yard that makes us think of Him; it is the graveyard that inspires solemn thoughts, for here we are amidst them who have breathed and lived with us, and who have solved the mystery of the hereafter, which it remains for us, sooner or later, to solve.

But, hark, here comes another funeral cortège. Here is the carriage of death containing all that remains of a human being — the poor clay — followed by the mourners. They are few. The chief mourner is a woman, robed in black — death's insignia. The marks of care and sorrow are indelibly impressed on her brow and face; no tears are in her eyes — she cannot weep. Her grief is too deep for tears — they are denied her. Does she grieve the less that she does not weep? No! no! Grief which can find vent in tears, finds relief. Grief which is hidden from all eyes save God's is all the more felt.

See! they stop. And now they take the coffin from the hearse and bear it along the pathway. The sun's rays fall on a little group standing around a new-made grave.

The holy words of God are solemnly spoken. The last look upon the face of the dead has been taken. The features are calm in their repose. He seems to be sleeping. This is death!

The lid of the coffin is screwed down, and the face is hidden forever. Slowly they lower the narrow, last home that he shall ever know. It is small; he wants no more. * * * It is done. The earth falls upon the coffin with a rattling sound; the grave-diggers hide it from sight. The mound is formed, the last dread ceremonies are over.

Silently the mourners turn. They have left him here. The rumbling sound of the carriage wheels dies out in the distance; all is silent again.

The moon is rising higher and higher; the sun is sinking deeper and deeper in the horizon.

All is quiet. He is at rest. No more suffering, no more care, no more anguish, no more passion. Death has conquered all. There is rest for him at last — rest in the grave.

See! the day is nearly spent; and as the king of light sinks behind the reddish, golden-hued clouds, his last rays fall upon the new-made grave, where reposes all that remains of him who was once known as James Farly.

CHAPTER XVII.

THE LION OF THE DAY.

FIVE years have passed since James Farly took his last look of "earth, and sun, and day," and Mary Farly, sitting alone at the window of this grand mansion, hears the sounds of laughter and mirth of the gay party enjoying themselves beneath her, and thinks of the past.

Her eyes are fixed on pale Luna, surrounded by her satellites, and sailing over the cloudless sky in all her soft brilliancy.

Five years have passed since her husband's death, and what has she accomplished towards the object for

which alone she lives ?   Nothing ! absolutely nothing !
All her endeavors to trace and discover Philip Marton,
since she has made her residence with the Dervilles,
have been in vain.   She is as far from him as ever,
and she has almost given up the search for him in
despair.   There is everything here to make her happy ;
they are all very attentive to her.   Poor May, who,
with the elasticity of youth, aided by the great con-
soler, Time, has recovered in great part from the
shadow which had threatened to blight her life forever,
clings to her with a daughter's affection.   Her every
wish has but to be expressed to be gratified.   She has
everything in the way of comfort that she can desire,
and yet she is not happy.   Her youth has passed away,
and she is growing old ; indeed, she looks years older
than she really is.   But the peace which she had hoped
to enjoy in her age is denied her.   The grave alone
offers her rest.   Yet she must live — live to redeem
Frederick Wyndham's name.   His life is gone ; it
cannot be given back to him.   All that she can do is
the mockery of removing the obloquy attached to his
name, and which otherwise always will be.

And here she sits alone, heedless of the gay party
dancing, laughing, joking, flirting, and amusing themselves beneath her.   These amusements have lost all
charms for her.   She has feigned an excuse to be left
alone.

The parlors are crowded with gay merry-makers of
both sexes ; for this is the night of May Derville's
party.

Her parents have done everything in their power to
keep her thoughts from dwelling on the sad fate of her

dead lover — and with partial success. They rightly thought she was young and might meet another to suit her fancy, and marry yet. Another person thought so, too.

But, see, the dance is over; and now, while some promenade up and down the spacious parlors, the others seat themselves and engage in conversation. They are all apparently enjoying themselves. But where is May? If you will come with us, you will see her, a shawl wrapped around her *petite* form, enjoying the evening air, and talking seriously with the attentive gentleman who sits by her side on the balcony — Mr. Charles Wilton.

Mr. Wilton is the "lion of the day," as they say in society. He has been paying his attentions to the young heiress for some time, and it is whispered that he is a favored one.

Bright and cultivated, able to converse on almost any subject, witty, sarcastic, polite, said to be wealthy, besides being handsome and a character in his way,— Mr. Charles Wilton was the centre of attraction wherever he graciously deigned to make an appearance.

Singular to say — for ladies' favorites are not generally liked by their own sex — Mr. Wilton was a favorite with everybody, ladies and gentlemen alike.

To May Derville he was an enigma. She both respected and admired him. He exercised over her a strange and utterly inexplicable influence. She liked to converse with him and draw out his opinions and ideas on various subjects ; and while she often differed with him, she always listened to his remarks with deference and attention.

I

"You ask me, Miss Derville," he was saying, "for my opinions in regard to religion. It is a subject which I never care to discuss, because it is unsusceptible of positive proof. I would rather, therefore, talk of anything else, unless, using a lady's prerogative, you insist."

"I would like to know what you think on the subject, very much, Mr. Wilton," she answered; "but, of course, if it is objectionable to you we will let it drop."

"I see you are too polite to insist, while you ardently desire to know," he said, smiling. "Am I not right?"

"I confess you are," she replied, frankly.

"As an Indian would say, Miss Derville, your tongue is straight."

"Thanks for the compliment. I always endeavor to speak plainly, though, I have been told, it is not always the best policy."

"When people speak out plainly, and say what they mean, my dear Miss Derville, all danger of a misunderstanding is avoided; and, therefore, as you desire it, I cannot be so ungentlemanly as to deny your request, for I am always happy when I can do anything for you. I know that, however ridiculous my opinion may appear to you, you will not laugh at me."

"You are very complimentary, Mr. Wilton; but you underrate yourself. You always speak so wisely and are so well informed on everything, that it gives me great pleasure to listen to you and try to comprehend, by means of the little brains I have, your meaning."

"You cannot take more pleasure in listening to me, Miss Derville, than I take in conversing with you. Ladies (excuse me for disparaging your sex) are, as a general rule, so frivolous and unable to say anything, — so false is the education they usually receive, — except about dress, fashion, and other kindred subjects, that most men of mind hesitate before saying anything to them of a serious nature. This is the reason why your scholar is not generally a ladies' man. But you, Miss May, are an exception to the rule. It is well to be able to suit one's self to the capabilities of every one; to be able to talk fashion, to say silly words, nonsense, little nothings, and to converse on serious, sober, intellectual subjects; it all depends on the person you are speaking with, and a man or woman who is able to suit himself, or herself, to others and to circumstances is pretty certain to be a general favorite."

" While I partly agree with you," said May, "I yet must differ. There are plenty of women who are just as capable as men; and while there are any number who are as you say, you must yet remember that the greater proportion of your own sex are no better. I repeat, then, that there are any number of women fully as capable as men, only — "

" Only, like the needle in the haystack, they are hard to find. But then, again, probably these capable women, I suppose, may have the same idea of my sex."

" The fault is more with the parents than with the children, I think, Mr. Wilton."

" In that regard you are, to a certain extent, right. The children of the poor in many cases are taken away from school at an early age, being compelled to work for a living, while others never go at all. The children of the rich, again, are often humored too much. A parent is apt to believe a child, without listening at all to the teacher. This works a vast amount of harm, for the teachers in a private, fashionable school, to which the greater number of wealthy people, especially if they be shoddies, send their children, or else have teachers at home, know that they are dependent upon their scholars, who are consequently apt to take advantage of their situation. For this reason I think public schools are greatly to be preferred. There is one thing, however, which I never thought proper, and that is the habit of making teachers presents. Not that I begrudge the teacher, whose life, at the best, is a hard one; but the poorer scholars, who are either unable or to whom it is a great burden to contribute to make the teacher a present, are, in a manner, looked down upon by their richer classmates, and favoritism is apt to be shown. Besides, it hurts the feelings of the poor, and we should always regard the feelings of others. There are a great many corrections needed in our present educational system, and the first remedy should be to make education compulsory."

"I agree with you there, Mr. Wilton."

"Another thing, Miss Derville. Children, especially young girls, are taken from school too early, and when their education is merely — if I may use the phrase — glossed over. They know a little of this, a little of that, and nothing perfect. They are taught too much at once; too much entirely. And in respect to young girls, they are too early, as the saying is, brought out. For instance, the other day I called on an old lady friend, whom I had not seen in some years, and there met her daughter, a young girl of, I should judge, seventeen. In the course of conversation, I remarked to the daughter, 'I suppose you have almost finished your studies?' She arose, apparently greatly insulted, and left the room. I was at a loss how to account for her strange behavior until her mother apologized for her, and told me that Cecilia was engaged. I was surprised. A young, child-looking girl, who could not possibly know her own mind and should have been at school, engaged to be married! Yes, it was true. Did she know what she was going to do? Had she any idea of the solemnity of marriage? Not the least. To her it was a great thing — a matter for the envy of others. She had been brought up in a fashionable school, where the only things taught were dress, fashion, and hurry-up-and-get-a-husband-or-you-will-be-an-old-maid. That was the great thing — don't be an old maid! How many unhappy married men and women there are in this city to-day, the result of such thoughtlessness, I need not tell you. People marry nowadays just as they would do anything of oh-nothing-at-all importance. Afterwards, when the romance of the affair is dispelled, they find that what they imagined love was merely fancy. I might say much more on this topic, but it is going away entirely from the subject we first broached. To return, then, to religion. Let me premise by informing you, that you may not deem me a hypocrite, that I do not pretend to be religious or to always practise what I preach; it is so much easier preaching than practising. When you ask me for my opinions

12

on religion, I tell you, not perhaps what I do, but
what I think proper and right. First, then, religion
is simply a matter of belief — of faith ; for without
faith, there can be no religion, but only hypocrisy.
There are any number of religious sects, each one
worshipping in its own peculiar way. They all, however, worship a being they term God ; so you see, it
all amounts to the same thing. Each day in the week
is a Sunday to some one of these sects — a day set
apart for the worship of a being termed God. Now,
it cannot be doubted that religion is a preventative of
crime. Were it certain that when a man dies, that is
the end of him, numberless men who now, through
fear of punishment hereafter, even if they escape here,
remain upright in action, if not in thought, would be
great criminals. Now, in every religion, whatever the
belief may be, I can find much that is good and much
that is bad ; and while religion has worked a vast
amount of good, it has also worked a vast amount of
bad — or, rather, I should say it is fanaticism that has
worked the bad ; but fanaticism has been the offspring
of religion, even if religion — that is, some beliefs —
do not teach it. No man has a right to say to another,
' You are wrong and I am right ; mine is the only true
religion ? ' Why, my dear Miss Derville, I know of a
case where, incredulous as it may appear to you, one
man said to another, ' My dear sir, I like you very
much — as much as any one I know — and I am sorry
for you, for you know you do not believe right and so
are doomed —' well, to say it politely, to go below
stairs, where the thermometer ranges well up in the
hundreds."

Miss Derville smiled. Mr. Wilton continued:
" Now, this man undoubtedly believed what he said
and thought himself religious. But was he? What
right had he to judge? Why could not the other have
said the same to him with equal propriety? What
right has either of them to say the other is wrong?
None, none, whatever. It is against the spirit of true
religion. No man has the right to say to another that
his religion is false. He cannot positively prove it; it
is simply a matter of belief. Am I right? "

" I think you are."

CHAPTER XVIII.

HOW CRIMINALS ARE MADE.

THIS question of religion, Miss Derville," continued
Mr. Wilton, " has puzzled greater minds than
mine. The more we discuss it, the more bewildered
we become. It is for this reason that I never care to
argue it. One who allows his thoughts to dwell on it
too much becomes morbid, perhaps fanatic, perhaps
insane. There is only one solution of it. We must
accept much that appears improbable without question
or inquiry. We can all believe what we choose; it
concerns ourselves, and is our own business. It is this
spirit of proclaiming ourselves right, and all who believe otherwise wrong, that has caused all the religious
persecutions history records, and has promoted atheism.
And I am pained to say that my experience has shown

me that even now, in what we call the nineteenth century of civilization, bigotry exists to an alarming extent, and sectarian prejudice is still very great. We
look on past ages as barbarous and uncivilized. Future
ages will look back on us in the same light, and just as
justly, for civilization never ceases, and the day is sure
to come when the entire world will be of one and the
same faith and belief as regards religion, and future
generations will wonder how we of to-day could ever
have been so diverse in our religious opinions, and yet
have called ourselves civilized, when bigotry existed
among us."

"Yes; that is doubtless true, Mr. Wilton. But,
pardon me if I interrupt you. Suppose we go back to
the starting-point, as we will be missed soon, if we are
not already, and you have not as yet told me what your
belief is."

"I will tell you first what I do not believe. I do
not believe in the man who keeps up to the strict tenets
of any religion, while, at the same time, he does not
believe in one-half of them. The world may call him
religious, because he attends church regularly; but I
call him a hypocrite. Hypocrites are detestable."

"Especially religious hypocrites."

"Well, then, Miss Derville, I consider a man religious who keeps up to those principles which appear
right to him, and who does what he thinks right —
not does so because he is told to, but because he believes
it right."

"I must differ with you there, Mr. Wilton, because
then the murderer might call himself religious, for he
could say he thought he was right."

"Ah! excuse me for telling you that you fall into a too common error. Let me ask you one question. Do you think it possible for a man to commit a crime, and say that he thought he was doing right?"

"Well —"

"Yes — excuse me for interrupting you, Miss Derville — he might say so, but would he believe it? could he convince himself that he honestly thought so?"

"Well, you know, Mr. Wilton, we can generally make ourselves believe whatever we wish to."

"That is partly true. But we often try to convince ourselves we are right, when we know and feel we are wrong. We try to quiet the inner voice. Now, I am going to ask you a startling question. For myself, I answer no. Do you believe in a hell?"

"No, I do not. Hell is our guilty conscience. It may sleep sometimes, but it must awake at last."

"But some people have no conscience."

"Do you think so? I do not. They try to make themselves believe they have it not, because it sleeps, and does not disturb them. But it must awake some time, and then they suffer the torments of hell."

Mr. Wilton smiled.

"That may and may not be," he said; "however, some people suffer so much on earth that it is impossible for them to suffer worse tortures hereafter."

"Why, the world is good."

"True — too good for the people who live in it. But now you have heard my views on religion, what think you of them?"

"I agree and I disagree. But talking of murderers, what think you of them?"

12 *

"When there is no crime, there will be no world. Crime seems to increase as civilization advances. Why, there are from twenty to thirty thousand professional law-breakers in this city to-day."

"As many as that?"

"Yes, fully. And the statistics show that this class is constantly increasing, and becoming greater in number, year after year."

"And what is the cause of this continual increase?"

"Poverty is one cause; and the richer the world becomes the greater poverty there is in it. But there are many causes which a lady cannot be told. How poverty is one cause can easily be explained. If we examine our criminal statistics, and the lives of probably one-half of our criminals, we will find this to be the case: Mr. R—— is a man in the middle class of life, in moderate circumstances. He becomes reduced, and very poor. In an unguarded moment he commits forgery, or a theft — perhaps to keep his family from starving. You see our law is so curious that a man who steals a loaf of bread is often more severely punished than one who takes life."

"I am very greatly interested. Please continue."

"Well, say even in a moment of passion he commits murder. He is arrested, tried, sent to prison for a number of years; or, in case of murder —"

"Suffers death."

"Exactly. The law punishes him; but not only him. His wife, his three young sons, aged between five and eight, and a daughter, say of four years, suffer for his crime also."

"It is hard; but it must be done."

"Wait; allow me one moment, please. Left without any one to support her or her family, too proud — for the poor as well as the rich are proud, Miss Derville — too proud to go to the almshouse, not willing to part with her children, and naturally feeling bitter against them who, as she says, ' knowing not poverty,' have deprived her of her only support — shunned, pointed at as the wife of a criminal, she can obtain no work, for no one will trust her — can you not imagine the sequel, Miss Derville, or shall I tell you?"

"I had rather you would tell me."

"She rebels against the law. The serpent is ever near, watching; the three young boys, and the little girl, from that time are brought up in an atmosphere of sin, with society's outcasts for companions; they come of age; what should be the happiest period of their lives gone, and themselves, though young in years, old in crime. In this manner the criminal classes receive three new males, and, who are infinitely more capable of doing mischief, two female members."

"What you tell me is horrible," said May, impressed by his manner quite as much as by his words.

"Truth is stranger than fiction, Miss Derville. What I have told you is true; I know it."

"But, Mr. Wilton, surely you would not have us allow criminals to escape all punishment, simply because they may happen to have wives and children?"

"Assuredly not; but I would have the law provide for the wives and children."

"Why, there are plenty of places —"

"But they are too proud to go to a public charity-house. The law should look after and care for them —

see that the children are properly educated. But I cannot explain my whole meaning to you, or my plans, just now. Some other time, if you desire it, I may. I will only say that the money this would require would be insignificant in comparison to the benefits society would derive from it."

"Well, I will not trouble you any further at present. Only one question more: Do you think a person could commit murder in cold blood?"

"Certainly I do. But, come, it is growing chilly. Allow me to escort you inside."

Arm in arm they entered the brilliantly lit up parlors, while all eyes were turned significantly on them.

Before retiring that night, May detailed to Mary Farly her whole conversation with Mr. Wilton.

"I cannot but agree with him in some respects," said Mrs. Farly. "I would like to see this man, who seems to be the lion of the day. But I cannot agree with him that a human being, possessed of a rational mind, and in full control of the senses with which God has endowed him, could commit murder in cold blood. The idea is, to me, at total variance, and incompatible with any opinion of human nature not in itself depraved and bad. The man may appear perfectly sane — may commit murder simply for money — yet his mind is to some degree diseased. But you should not think of such subjects, May; you should enjoy your life."

"Yes," thought May, "that is always it. We should be happy, and not give a thought to the miserable, or for their welfare. I know Mary does not mean that; but such is the opinion and advice of the world."

CHAPTER XIX.

ALICE.

IF the outside of this tenement-house is miserable in the extreme, and seems to be hesitating whether to tumble down or remain standing, the inside is not much better. It is literally swarming with human beings, from the prattling child to the decrepit old woman.

In one room sits a woman plainly attired. There is a sad look in the deep blue eyes, and the marks of suffering are plainly discernible on the face. It is apparent that her life has not been a smooth one, and that, as she sits idly here, she must once have been very beautiful. Her beauty has not entirely faded yet. Evidently she is expecting a visitor and has nerved herself for a bitter struggle.

"I love him! I love him so!" she murmurs. "He cannot, oh, he must not desert me! No! no!"

Presently the room door opens, and a man enters into the wretched apartment. He advances towards her with open arms, as if expecting her to fly into them. But he is disappointed. She does half arise, as if to give way to her inclination; then, as some bitter memory comes to her, she sinks back into the chair and allows her hands to drop idly upon her lap.

A look of surprise is in his eyes as he bends over to kiss her; but she turns her face away and motions him off with her hands. His look changes into one half of fright and half of pain.

"Why, Alice!" he says, reproachfully.

But she only straightens herself up, looks him full in the face, and says simply — but, oh! so bitterly:

"So you have come!"

"Alice!"

There is a twinge of pain in his voice that touches her. For a moment she seems ashamed of the cold way in which she is treating him; and then, recovering from the almost irresistible impulse to rush to him and cry on his breast, she steadies her nerves again.

"Be seated," she says, curtly, motioning him to a chair.

"Alice, what's got over you? Is this the way you treat me? And you said you loved me! Is this the reception I am accorded from you?"

A bitter struggle takes place within her upheaving bosom; a wave of passion sweeps over her, and then— is gone.

"I despise you!" she says; but the words almost choked her.

The look of pain deepens in his eyes. His voice trembles as he speaks.

"You! Alice, you! you say that to me? Very well. I am going. Farewell!"

He turns around, places his hand on the knob of the door, then faces her again, and repeats:

"Farewell, Alice."   .

He half opens the door. She seems to be in a trance; but, suddenly, she rises, rushes to his side, grasps his arm, and says, hoarsely:

"Stay, John, stay!"

He makes a movement as if to clasp her in his arms.

At the action she conquers her emotion, steps back and says, commandingly :

"Sit down; I have much to say to you."

He obeys her in a bewildered manner, as if puzzled, and at a loss how to account for her strange conduct.

She closes and locks the door, and then comes and stands in front of him.

"Alice," he says, "your conduct is utterly inexplicable to me."

"Then listen to me, John," she replies, "and see if it is not justified. Look at me. Look at the wreck I am. I was young, and pure, and beautiful, they said, when I first met you. I loved you, John, and you told me that you loved me. I, poor fool, believed you; I believed in all your promises : I obeyed you, and did what you wished. I would have thought any sacrifice easy to have won your love. God pity me! I left home and parents, friends, for your sake; I lost honor; I became a social outcast for your sake. All these sacrifices willingly I made because I loved you; and, in my blindness, I thought you loved me —"

"Why, Alice —" he interrupted.

"Wait, and hear me through," she said, in a voice that trembled slightly with passionate emotion. "Only a few short years ago I was pure, I was happy, I was beloved; now I am lost, I am miserable, I am unloved!"

It is impossible to describe the tone in which the last words were said. It was full of a hopeless despair.

"Alice!" he interrupts again, and the one word speaks volumes.

"Oh, John!" she continues, unheeding his interruption, "I gave up everything that made life dear for your sake — because you promised to marry me. Day and night I have worked and slaved for you. I have tried to make you happy; I have done everything you asked of me — because I was to be your wife."

"And so you will be, Alice."

"So I will be! How often you have said those words to me! How can I believe you? Will you come and marry me now?"

"Alice, you doubt me. Oh, Alice! you doubt me; and I have been working all these years for you. No, no — you do not love me."

Either the man felt what he said, or else he was a consummate actor.

"Oh, John, do not say that! do not say that! You know I love you!" she cried, giving away to her feelings at last. "But why not marry me now? It would make me so much happier."

"Alice, I cannot at present." At the words she regained her self-possession.

"Yes!" she said, sternly, bitterly. "That is always your answer — Not at present! And meanwhile you are plotting to rid yourself of me; meanwhile you are paying your attention to others, and I am deserted; I am cast off like an orange out of which all the juice has been sucked."

He whistled — a long, prolonged whistle, that told he had discovered the cause of her strange conduct.

"Oh, ho!" he laughed. "Why, Alice, jealous! Now, now, my pretty girl, jealous! Why, Alice!"

"Jealous!" she cried, passionately. "Have I not

cause to be jealous? I tell you that I love you; I love you who has ruined me, and you shall not desert me! No, no, never! never while I live!"

"Now, Alice, if you are through, probably you will give me a chance to explain," he said, quietly. "It is useless getting into a passion; it does no good. Besides, you do not know what you say in your anger, and may repent it. Come, sit down by me, and listen!"

She obeyed him.

"Now, Alice, I want to make a fortune, so that when we marry we can enjoy ourselves. You are a good girl and have done all that I have asked of you. I have always tried to please you — "

"And yet you go there day after day of late, and I am left alone!"

"Now, Alice, don't be jealous! If I go there, it is for your sake. Never mind. Some day you will thank me for it. I go to see her father on business, and cannot avoid seeing her; and yet here you are, jealous of me. Come now, Alice, be a sensible girl, and make it all up."

If he was lying, his lies had the tone of truth.

She flung her arms passionately around his neck, and kissed him over and over again.

"Oh, John, forgive a poor, miserable creature like me, who loves you so," she sobbed. "It was cruel in me to doubt you; but I loved you, John, and I could not bear to think of parting with you."

"There, there, my little girl! don't let it worry you. Don't cry, Alice; I love you; I shall not leave you. Only have faith in me."

13 K

"Oh, yes, John, I will!" she replied, and a smile of happiness was in her eyes that lit up her countenance with a holy look. Poor, poor thing! Well might she have said with the poetess:

> And darest thou speak of faithlessness and him
> In the same idle breath? Thou little knowest
> The strong confiding of a woman's heart
> When woman loves as — I do.

CHAPTER XX.

A CHANCE MEETING.

IT was a habit which Mary Farly had formed, since she had found a home with the Dervilles, of making once a week, regularly, a charity excursion; that is, having found out a number of worthy families in straitened circumstances, she took them in charge, and saw that they were provided for, and many were the heartfelt blessings showered on her head.

Hers was true charity, simple and secret. She did not believe in charity that was ostentatious; for, as she said, while it doubtless did a great deal of good, it was not true charity.

"The man or woman," she was wont to say, "who finds out a number of poor, worthy people and assists them to the extent of his or her ability, is far more charitable, in the true sense of the word, than they who erect large buildings, so that it may become known, and refuse assistance to the poor who come begging to their doors. While these people do good, their object, in almost every instance, is not charity, but self."

In these excursions she was generally accompanied by May; they served to keep her thoughts from resting on herself; but on this day, one week after the event related in the last chapter, we see her setting out alone.

We do not mean to detail her many visits, or the welcome and blessings she received. These poor, simple people regarded her in their enthusiasm as a guardian angel, and could not imagine that she was a human being like themselves, and that she was poorer and more miserable in many respects than even they were.

It was late in the day, when, on her mission of love, she entered the miserable tenement mentioned in the preceding chapter. There lived in this wretched place one family who were the recipients of her charity.

It was after she had attended to their welfare, and had descended the stairs and stood at their foot on the landing, that a door in front of her opened, and a man emerged into the entrance-way and passed hurriedly out. His exit was followed by the sound of a fall and sobbing.

Probably these sounds were of such frequent occurrence that none of the miserable inmates of this wretched habitation saw anything unusual in them, or paid any attention to them. Misery and poverty go hand-in-hand together; and people have enough troubles of their own without attending to others'. At least this seemed to be the motto here. But to Mary

Farly these sobs seemed to come from a breaking heart, and she could not resist the temptation to inquire into their cause, and comfort the miserable being from whom they came, if that were possible.

It was well for her that she did so, and it was by one of those strange fatuities that can only be accounted for as Providential that she entered the room from whence the sobs seemed to come.

It was a miserable place; but the sight that attracted Mary Farly's attention was not the wretchedness and poverty that was everywhere visible, but a woman, who had slipped from off the miserable apology for a chair, and with her face buried in her hands knelt and sobbed as though her heart was breaking. Her form shook like a reed in the wind, and her moans seemed as though they could have melted a heart of stone with pity.

"Ah, me!" murmured the sympathetic intruder. "Misery, misery everywhere! None so poor, but others are poorer."

Then she advanced and laid her hand on the miserable creature's shoulder gently.

"My poor woman," she said, "don't cry so. I am your friend. Tell me what I can do to comfort you."

But the woman's sobs only came the faster and more hysterically.

"Leave me alone," she moaned. "Oh! leave me alone. I wish I was dead! oh! I wish I was dead!"

"No, no, my poor woman; don't say so. Don't talk so wildly. It is wrong, it is wicked to wish yourself dead. Come, calm yourself. Look up, and let me comfort you."

"No! no! I am miserable! Oh! I am so miserable! There is no comfort for me here; there is no comfort for me!"

"There is comfort for all who do not refuse it. Come, let me be your friend; won't you?"

Perhaps it was the sincere tone in which the words were said, or perhaps it was an instinctive feeling that the speaker was really a friend, that caused the woman to suddenly hush her sobbing, and look up at Mary Farly.

As their eyes met, they both started with a movement of violent astonishment. One look — but one — and they were locked in each other's embrace.

"Alice!"

"Mary!"

That was all that passed between them for some minutes.

They had met — met for the first time since the happy hours, long, long ago, when they had known each other as school-girls. These two women — who had known each other in better, happier days, when life had been a pleasant dream; when they, as classmates and loving friends, had romped together in the old school-yard, and who had lost sight of each other during many long years which had intervened since the happy days of their girlhood — met again, but, oh! in what different circumstances! — met again, but under what a different aspect!

Those had been days of happiness and affluence; but now, oh! now, what a change!

Who can tell what the impenetrable future holds in store for us?

13 *

And so they had met — these two, who had known each other as girls; who had speculated on the future; who had laughed, and played, and romped together; who had compared their thoughts, and unfolded their plans, and entrusted their little secrets to each other — these two, whose lives had opened so auspiciously, and under such bright aspects; for whom the future had seemed to hold only happiness; whose life-paths had diverged, but who had both trodden the thorny path, met again as — women.

There was much to be told, much to be said on both sides. But it was Alice who, after they had recovered from their surprise, and had become familiar again, first told the history of her life since they had last seen each other.

Can it not be guessed? It was nothing new, nothing strange; the same old, every-day story, that, alas, is so familiar to almost every one. Who has not heard that old story,

> So old, so old,
> So often told,

— the story of a pure, trusting heart, which loved not wisely, but too well — the story of

> The cat and dove —
> Of man's deceit, and woman's love?

There is no need of repeating it here.

"Last night," she concluded, while a burning blush suffused her cheeks, "he was here. Oh, Mary, I had never seen him so before. He was always temperate, calm, collected — never in a passion; but last night something must have disturbed him greatly, for he did

what he never had done before — talked in his sleep.
I heard every word he said, and, oh, how they crushed
me! He was planning to rid himself of me. I was
a burden to him — I, who had done so much, and
would do even more, if it were possible, for his sake.
Oh! Mary, you cannot imagine what I felt! He said
he must rid himself of me; that she loved him, and
he would marry her, and so become rich; that his
plans must succeed. To-day, we had a quarrel, and
he has left me in anger. Oh! Mary, Mary, what shall
I do? What shall I do?"

She sobbed hysterically again.

"Come, now, Alice," said Mary Farly, soothingly,
"don't give way so. Cheer up, for my sake. Tell me
who this girl is, and I will see her; and if she is at all
honorable, she will let him go."

"No, oh, no; he would blame me for it; he would
hate me!" moaned the unfortunate woman.

"He need never know, Alice, who told her. Be a
brave woman, and tell me who she is."

"I will tell you her name. She is rich, she is happy,
she is far above me. But you must promise me that,
whatever may come, you will shield him from harm."

"What! Alice, you love him still? And after
what he has done to you? You love him still, and he
so unworthy?"

She bowed her head, and answered in a low voice:

"I love him still. Don't chide me, don't blame me,
don't ask me why; I only know I love him; I always
will love him while I live."

Yes, she loved him. This man had betrayed, had
ruined her; had blasted her life, and made her an out-

cast; this man had made of her the miserable being she was, and yet she loved him. It mattered not what he had done, she loved him. Is it not strange that a woman's best affections, a woman's love should be lavished on so unworthy an object; that she should cling to him who had ruined her, and robbed her of all that made life worth the having? But who can account for that most strange and inexplicable of all passions — Love?

"She speaks the truth," Mary Farly said pityingly to herself. "She loves him still."

"But, Alice," she said aloud, "you must tell me — you owe it to yourself to tell me, if you know — the name of this girl. You owe it to her."

"I know it; I know it. But I cannot, oh, I cannot, have harm come to him through me!"

"Alice, you are foolish. I insist upon knowing this girl's name!"

"Promise me, then," begged the miserable woman, "that no harm shall come to him. Promise me that you will shield him from all danger, all harm."

"I promise you, Alice, that I will do all in my power to help him, though he is so unworthy. I will do it for your sake."

The woman recovered her composure.

"I believe you, Mary," she said. "I will trust you, and tell you her name."

"What is it?"

"May Derville!"

Can we portray the astonishment of Mary Farly?

"May — May Derville!" she exclaimed. "Are you sure?"

"I am."

This necessitated a short explanation from Mary Farly. It was now Alice's turn to be surprised.

"You live there?" she exclaimed; "You live with them? Oh! then you have seen him. Promise me you will not harm him."

"I have already given you my promise, Alice. But you forget that I do not see one-half of the gentlemen who visit her, and you have not told me his name."

"He passes under the name of Charles Wilton, I believe."

"Charles Wilton!"

What! the pet of society; the elegant, accomplished, admired Charles Wilton? Was she dreaming, or did she hear aright? Was it this man — could it be this man who had ruined her girlhood's friend? There was no room for doubt; she was not dreaming; she had heard aright.

Strange! the many and various palpable contradictions of human nature! But, then, had not Mr. Charles Wilton himself said that he suited himself to others, and to circumstances? and that it was easier preaching, than practising?

This was a day of surprises; but the greatest one was yet in store for her.

She hid her feelings as best she could from her companion, and said, calmly:

"You say he passes under the name of Charles Wilton?"

"Yes."

"I have heard of him. What is his true name?"

"I knew him first as John Brady; but I know he

has passed under many names at different times, and if that be his right name or not, I cannot tell."

"Can you tell me some of the names he has been known by, Alice?"

"Yes. Before I knew him I have ascertained that he used the names of William Johnson, Charles Williams, and Philip Marton."

Was it a wonder that Mary Farly started so violently in astonishment?

"Charles Williams — Philip Mar — Mar—!" she gasped.

"Philip Marton," repeated Alice, looking on in silent amazement.

Mary Farly trembled like an aspen. The room reeled before her eyes, and she came near fainting. The shock was almost too great.

She had found him! found him after years of patient wearing, watching, and searching — found him, and by a mere accident!

What great things — what great discoveries have been the result of just such simple accidents?

She had searched, and searched, and hunted for this man for years without success, but to find him at last by a mere chance-meeting.

"God moves in a mysterious way his wonders to perform," she thought, when she had recovered her composure somewhat.

"You know something," Alice exclaimed, in alarm. "Tell me — what is it?"

Should she tell her? No! she would spare her that. She had promised not to harm him, and she would be true to her word if he would do what she would ask of him — and he must. He should not escape her now — now, when God had given her her reward; when, as by a miracle, he had been delivered up to her.

"It's nothing, Alice," she replied; "I am subject to these spells."

"I have found you," she thought. "At last! at last!"

CHAPTER XXI.

CAUGHT.

THE elegant Mr. Charles Wilton, attired becomingly in the height of fashion, and twirling a short, plain-looking cane between his fingers, ascended the dignified-looking stoop, and pulled the silver-plated bell-knob.

The girl who opened the door stood as if entranced for a moment at sight of him; the look on his face was full of such a quiet resolve and self-complacency.

"Is Miss Derville in?" he inquired, removing his hat with gentlemanly politeness.

"If you will walk in the parlor, please, sir, I will see," she answered.

The elegant Mr. Wilton walked into the sumptuous parlors, while the girl ascended the stairs and knocked at the room-door on the second floor.

Three women were in the room, all pale, and seemingly in suspense — May, Alice, and Mary Farly.

"Mr. Wilton," announced the girl, and withdrew.

Poor Alice came near fainting.

"Courage!" said Mary Farly to her. "Be brave and ready when I call. Do not let your fortitude desert you."

The elegant Mr. Wilton meanwhile, sitting in expectation in the parlor, heard the hall-door open and close, and a few moments later, a woman whom he did not know — Mary Farly — appeared before him.

He arose politely, rather disappointed.

Be careful, now, Mr. Wilton! You will need all your assurance to support you; you have to battle with a woman!

"Mr. Wilton, I believe," she said, calmly, "I have often heard Miss Derville speak of you."

Mr. Wilton bowed.

"I am highly flattered by Miss Derville's notice," he said; "but, madam, is she out?"

"She is not well, sir, and sent me in her stead. Be seated, please."

He seated himself.

"I have often wished to meet you, sir," she continued, watching him narrowly. "My name is Mary Farly."

As a rule, this man had complete control over himself: but that name, so fraught with bitter recollections, was one that he had not forgotten; and it came so by surprise and so unexpectedly upon him, that he could not suppress his astonishment.

His first feeling was fear. He was tempted to fly. But, apparently, she was not paying him any attention; and so he restrained himself. Did this woman know him? Impossible! It was an accident merely — a chance-meeting.

He mumbled over some undistinguishable words, and then sat perfectly still, though his heart was beating violently.

"I have often heard you were a learned man, Mr. Wilton," she said, calmly, "and I have come to ask your advice. I have a short story to tell you."

She recounted to him James Farly's confession. His face became livid in hue — all this was so unexpected and startling! He looked at her. She was not noticing him; no, she did not know him. He must be calm.

"You see," she concluded, "I have promised not to harm him, unless he forces me to extreme measures. Now, what shall I do?"

Somewhat reassured, he answered as calmly as possible under the circumstances:

"Having found this man, madam, you ought to see him, and compel him to do what you desire."

She arose and drew a small table — on which was pen, ink, and paper — in front of him!

He sat still and motionless — half paralyzed; he could not have stirred one step at that moment.

"Then," she said, firmly, "Mr. Charles Wilton, *alias* Charles Williams, *alias* Philip Marton, write a confession of the part you enacted in the murder of Leslie Wyndham!"

He remained motionless; no chains could have bound him more securely to his seat.

"Madam!" burst from his pale lips, "I — I — do not — understand you!"

"Come, sir," she said, firmly as before, "I have no time to waste. Be wise and write!

14

"Madam!" he stammered again, "I — I — you mistake — "

"I do not mistake, sir; I know you! Alice!"

At the call the woman entered. She was deathly pale, and trembling.

At sight of her his color seemed to turn to a ghastly green. For perhaps the first time in his life he lost all his self-possession. He was lost! Caught, at last, by a woman!

What followed was the work of an instant — was like a flash of lightning.

"You!" he exclaimed, in the same tone that Cæsar may be supposed to have said *"Et tu Brute"* in, as the woman he had ruined advanced, with outstretched arms, towards him.

His passion was terrible to behold. His cane seemed to part, something bright flashed in the light, and, like a wounded tiger, he sprang towards her.

The next instant he stood as in a trance, while the blood spurted from her bosom; she staggered and fell at his feet, a heavenly look on the wasted face, that made it appear divine in its expression.

"John! oh, John!" she gasped. "You have killed me! you have killed me! and I love you still! Mary, Mary, God help him! I was wrong! oh, I was wrong! Oh, John, I forgive you, I forgive you!"

And so she died. Never another word left her lips; her last words were of him, — a prayer for the pardon of the man who had so cruelly wronged her.

And there he stood, motionless, powerless, bereft of all his senses.

A shriek burst from Mary Farly's lips at sight of

this awful, unexpected denouement; the sound of hurried footsteps were on the stairs; then two policemen entered the room where the tragedy had just taken place, and took him off, unresisting, speechless.

CHAPTER XXII.

TO THE WORLD.

THE news of the tragedy "at Derville's," and the arrest of Mr. Charles Wilton, occasioned the greatest excitement and astonishment. The wildest rumors for a time prevailed. The elegant Mr. Wilton, the pet of society, the man who had been courted and admired by the "Upper Ten," a common murderer? Yes, it was true. Society had received and admired and fostered a common criminal! How could society take revenge on this man who had made a dupe of it but by turning its back upon him? Society did so; and Mr. Wilton had many enemies who had feared him in his days of power, who, now that he was down, determined to keep him down.

Mary Farly visited him often, and prayed, begged, beseeched him to write a confession of the part he had acted in the murder of Leslie Wyndham; but he persistently denied and refused. Hope was not dead in his breast yet. But whatever hopes he may have entertained of escape, they were soon blasted. He went back to his cell one day condemned to death.

She visited him a few days before the time appointed

for the carrying out of the dread sentence of the law.

"There is no hope for you," she said, "and I am sorry for you. Your life is drawing to a close, and whatever you may do cannot make your name (believe me, I do not mean to wound your feelings) more ignominious than it now is. I ask you, I beg of you, as a last act of justice, as one good act of your life, to grant my wishes. It cannot injure you; it will make me feel more at rest."

"See here," he answered, after a few moments, pause, "I have no cause to thank you, for but for you I would not be here to-day; and yet I admire you for your pluck and courage. I cannot help it, and I will do what you desire, on one condition."

"Name the condition," she replied, "and if I can, I will perform it."

He whispered it to her. She recoiled as if a serpent had struck her.

"Well, as you wish," he said, nonchalantly.

She thought. She knew that what he asked of her was wrong; but was she wrong in agreeing to his conditions, in view of the end to be attained thereby?

She did agree, and promised not to make it public until one year after his death; and the confession was duly made and witnessed.

On the day named for the execution, the jailer, upon entering his cell, found him cold and still — dead!

"Committed suicide!"

No one could tell how or who had furnished him with the means. There remained but the bare fact that he had committed the last terrible act in a long career of crime.

There he lie — dead! by his side, one hand almost resting on it, a pile of manuscript, evidently just completed, for the ink with which his name had been signed was not quite dry, the first words of which, written in large letters, attracted the jailer's attention.

He took it up with a shudder, gave an alarm, and then proceeding to his private office began to read the suicide's last words. The manuscript ran thus:

TO THE WORLD!

How I became a Criminal.

Perhaps, what I am about to write may be the means of saving many who are now standing on the threshold of crime, the doors of which, always open, are only waiting to close on them, from coming to the miserable end which stares me in the face; perhaps, even my life, my death, may teach the world a lesson of incalculable benefit, — may prove to have been far better for it than the life of its best and purest man.

My mother, in her youth, must have been exceedingly beautiful, for even at the age of forty, despite all the trouble she had then passed through, I remember that she was a handsome woman. But she had not beauty alone to recommend her. She was well educated, talented, and the only child of wealthy parents, whose pride was even greater than their riches.

Of course, she had many lovers. She could have taken her choice from the richest and highest, in point of social standing, young men in the city.

14 *   L

Among these admirers of hers were two, whom I will call Albert Crompton and Philip Martindale. Were I to name the former, the memory of an old man who occupied a prominent position in what is, it has often seemed to me satirically, called Society, would suddenly cease to be cherished. He was, at the time of which I write, rich, — in fact, it had been his good fortune to be born in the lap of luxury, — but far from attractive. Martindale, on the other hand, possessed a fascinating exterior, was very talented, and very *poor !* Such is chance, and so does fortune divide her favors. Is the division equal? Not by any means. To be poor, in those days was, and in these is, to be guilty of a monstrous crime.

With the parents, Crompton, it may easily be divined, was the favorite. To have him for a son-in-law was the pinnacle of their ambition. Indeed, between him and Martindale they showed no favoritism. Favoritism? Why, the very idea was ridiculous! What was Martindale anyway? Who was he? Only a poor secretary! Surely, he could never dream of aspiring to the hand of the rich man's daughter? The rich man never thought of such a thing. But Martindale did! He forgot that love was not made for poor people. What right has a poor man to love? If you saw a man put a stone around his neck to drag him *down,* when he wished to go *up,* what would you call him? A fool? The word is not half forcible enough.

Well, it was the old story. The rich man's daughter loved the rich man's poor secretary, made what is termed a *mesalliance,* and was disowned by her parents.

The poor man had love, and expected to do wonders with it. He made a *mesalliance* too; in fact, he was guilty of a crime: for, if any apology can be made for poor people marrying at all, surely none can be found for a poor man who takes a girl accustomed to luxury to a home of poverty. Such a man is guilty of a crime.

Martindale soon found out his mistake. It is not to be expected that a girl accustomed to having her every wish gratified can endure poverty, and not grumble. There may be an exceptional case, but in the great majority the woman is sure to regret the step she has made. This is only human nature, — nothing more, — and this was the case with the secretary's wife. Not that there was any positive outbreak, — any great quarrels. No; but there were, frequently, murmurings of discontent, and petulant words, and sad looks, which spoke only too plainly, and cut poor Martindale to the heart.

He saw that he had cause to regret the rashness of his love. He saw that he had done wrong.

"Her I love best I have injured most," he said to himself. "I, a poor man, had no right to marry; and if I must have married, I should not have chosen outside of my own circle."

Thus, at times, my mother heard him soliloquize. But still, however, they were for a while, on the whole, comparatively happy. So long as he had only himself and wife to support, Martindale managed to get along — and that was all. But, alas! he added a third crime to his list. His first crime was poverty; his second, marrying; his third and greatest, bringing

children into the world. For what right has a man
who finds it out of his power to keep himself and wife
comfortably to bring innocent beings to life to share
in his misery? What justification can he offer for
thus entailing misery and suffering on others who are
powerless to prevent it? Is it not a crime?

I asked a question above, viz., What would you
think of a man who puts a stone around his neck to
drag him down, when he wished to go up? Suppose,
now, that man kept on putting stones around his neck,
what would you think of him then? Can you find a
word expressive enough? Yet this was just what
Martindale did. This was his third crime; for, surely,
if, as I hold, a man has no right to marry unless he
knows that he can keep his wife comfortably, much
less has he a right to have children. This is my theory;
the practice is very different; for it seems to me that
the poorer the people the larger the family. A poor
man has no end of children; a rich man usually has
but few.

Martindale had six—four girls and two boys, one of
whom was myself. Two of the girls died in babyhood;
died from want of proper care — from want of proper
nourishment. What could my parents do? They
worked hard enough, God knows! But with eight
mouths to feed on the starvation wages of two people,—
how could it be done properly? My mother was proud,
and so was my father, — so proud that they would rather
have died than have asked for charity.

Things grew worse and worse. With the desperation of despair my parents struggled along. They
gave their children love; they did all they could for

their offspring. No one knew how we managed to live at home. My father, proud as the richest and greatest, kept up a semblance of what is called "appearances"—such it was for people living in a crowded, dirty tenement. We were starving gradually, but no one knew it.

Our co-tenants, poor and miserable themselves, managed to eke out an existence, and imagined we were doing the same. They never knew how hard things were with us — how we lived. Lived? It was no life. We did not live. We only kept on *dying*.

My father, understanding the worth of a good education, determined that his children should never have cause to blame him for not giving them one. And so, despite his poverty, he kept us at school, working the harder to sustain existence. At first he tried authorship. This did not succeed. He could not publish his own works, and publishers returned them "respectfully declined." And yet his works were far superior to the majority of those issued. But he was unknown in the world of letters, and he could not get an opening and receive compensation for his labor.

"There is no encouragement of home talent in America," he used to say. "Foreign authors sell here; American talent is dying for want of nourishment. We have just as great writers here as in any part of the world, — unknown men, who, if they could but be heard, would make a lasting name. It is easy enough saying that a publisher will take anything if it is good, but let an unknown man, without money and friends, try to secure a publisher in his own country, and see what will be the result."

I have said that my father's works were good. How
do I know? Because a play which he wrote was stolen
by the Manager to whom he sent it, and produced with
great success. What could my father do? Nothing!
His work was not copyrighted; he had no proof — no
witness but himself; he had no money to spend in
law, — he was helpless.

I was sixteen when I graduated. My brother, who
was not at all inclined to study, had left previously,
and was working on a small salary. My sisters were
yet at school.

I procured a situation down town at the enormous
salary of four dollars a week, and so, for a while, between us four — my brother, father, mother, and myself, — we managed to live a little better than we had
been accustomed to.

One day, my mother met her old lover, Albert
Crompton, in the street. She was still handsome,
despite the trouble she had known, and the sight of
her lit up the old flame in his breast. He had not forgotten or forgiven her; he still remembered her with
a mad passion, — a passion altogether, or nearly so,
sensual. When she married my father, it had been
a great blow to him. From that moment he had
nourished a hatred against my father — a fierce, bitter,
vindictive hatred.

The sight of my mother, whom he had not seen in
some years, revived his mad passion, and all the old
bitter memories which had never been quite dead.

He immediately instituted inquiries and learnt all
about us; found out how poor we were, and then, as I
afterwards learnt from her own lips, made her an in-

famous proposal. She immediately rejected it, with words of scathing scorn, and he left her, breathing vengeance.

That night, when my father came home, I noticed that he was unusually downcast. The truth came out. He had been discharged by his employer. When he asked for a reason, the only answer he received was, that "business was dull, and expenses must be curtailed."

The following day my brother came home — discharged. My father and he endeavored to procure other situations, — vainly. Manual labor was not in their sphere; they were not strong enough, — and no other could be got.

The whole support of the family fell on my mother and myself. We worked like slaves, and I saw with pain that her strength and health were breaking down from over-work, over-taxation.

I was, naturally, exceedingly ambitious. I dreamt of fame and greatness, and my leisure hours I had spent in the composition of a work which was to gain them for me. My hopes in this respect were blasted. My attempt at authorship met with the same fate as my father's had, previously. Oh! the cruelty of that "respectfully declined!" If they had read my work, I would not have heeded it so much; but I knew that it had not even been looked at, for I received it back, unopened, on the same day on which I had left it. I had gone to the publisher's full of hope, — dreaming of the happiness which I was about to give my father and mother — thinking that I would be able, alone, to support the family. Alas! my hopes were blasted. I felt that day that darkness had closed in all around me ; I looked into the future and saw nothing bright,— nothing to encourage me. I blamed my father for ever bringing me into the world — I blamed him, in my selfishness, for being poor. My brain whirled as I thought of what I could do, if I only had money! I looked at my mother working like a slave; I looked at my father, a stony expression of despair in his eyes; I looked at my brother (who had, at last, secured a situation as copyist on a salary of six dollars a week), moody and silent, and full of a bitterness which he could not conceal, and my sensitive nature received a shock to think that I could not do anything to help them. Oh! I felt the cruel stings of poverty then if ever a human being did! Had I been alone, I knew that in time I would rise; but with others to look after, I had no chance.

That day another misfortune befell us. The factory at which my mother worked failed, and all hands were thrown out of employment.

I looked at my father when he heard the news, and I saw a fierce resolve in his eyes that appelled me. I could not make out the expression ; I could only see that he had formed some desperate resolve—that he was frenzied. Had he not trouble enough to frenzy him ? He was a husband who loved his wife ; — he saw himself unable to support her, when he would have died to have made her happy. He was a father who loved his children ; — he saw them deprived of the necessaries of life. John, my brother, made six dollars a week ; he managed, by doing odd work which galled his pride, and day by day shortened his life by years, to make eight, and I made four — eighteen dollars a week, now that my mother's work had failed, was all there was to support a family of six!

He sat up late that night. He did nothing but write, write, write. He was out of the house early on the following morning. When I came home, I saw him sitting there like a statue. He seemed to be in a state of great nervousness. The least sound startled him—at the opening of a door, the fall of a footstep, he started.

My mother called me aside, — I was her confidant always, — and showed me a hundred dollar bill.

"Your father brought this home to-day," she said, "and gave it to me saying, that he had borrowed it from an old friend, who was going to give him profitable employment, and telling me to give the children a treat for once in their lives." And then she added, in a whisper, "I fear he has done something wrong!"

And so he had. That night he was arrested. In his desperation he had forged a check on his old employer. My mother gave the money up. She could not blame him. She realized his position ; she saw that he had done it for our benefit. * * * He was found dead in his cell in the morning. He had died during the night — died of the shame and disgrace. He had committed the crime to benefit us ; the effect was the contrary. This was the result : the shock threw my mother on a sick bed, John and I were discharged at the end of the week, — we were the sons of a criminal, and his sin was visited upon us, — *his* eight dollars, which had gone far to our support, was now lost, and starvation stared us in the face.

15

When I entered the room on that Saturday night,—
four days after my father's death,—I saw Crompton
there. Oh! what a terrible temptation he was holding
out to my mother! If she yielded, her children would
be removed from the danger of starvation. I think
she was on the point of yielding when I entered the
room, but the sight of me checked her. She ordered
him out of the house. He saw, then, that as long as I
was with her he had nothing to hope.

On Monday morning, sick as she was, my mother
went out in search of work, and John and I followed
her example. Well, there is no use in detailing how
we managed for the next six months. As soon as
people found out who we were,—and somehow or
another they learnt it in a few days,—perhaps, Crompton had something to do with it,—we were discharged.
No one would trust the wife and children of a criminal.

We were born proud; we endured everything, rather
than ask for charity. No one inquired about us; no
one paid any attention to our welfare.

The climax came at last. One night John failed to
come home, and that same night my mother was pros-
trated. She had been fasting for two days; my little
sisters had been fasting for two days; I had been fasting for two days. And we had not a cent.

I heard my sisters crying for something to eat; I
saw my mother lying sick and helpless, moaning for
bread for her little ones, and I powerless to give them
what they asked. My brain whirled, and my heart
sank with despair. Oh! the agony I endured.

I could stand it no longer. Bread! bread! I must
have bread!

I dashed out into the street, mad with despair! I ran against a man. I saw that he held a watch in his hand. Before he was aware of my purpose, I had it in my possession; before he could recover from his astonishment, I had disappeared from his sight. He had caught a glance of my face; that was all. I did not give myself time to think. I rushed into a pawn-shop. The pawnbroker knew me; I had been in his place often before to pledge what little jewelry my mother had kept. He advanced me a pittance, — the two-hundreth part of the value of the watch. Never mind; it was enough. It would buy bread; it would buy a little something — something delicate — for my sick mother.

I brought them home something to eat. I saw them devour it with avidity. Not even my mother thought to ask me any questions. I saw her eyes light up at the sight of the little girls eating. I saw her satisfying the hunger that was gnawing at her vitals. I could not eat. She clasped me in her arms; she pressed me to her breast; she called me her darling, and my heart was too choked for utterance.

Suddenly there came a knock on the door. I started with fear. The sense of what I had done rushed over me with the rapidity of lightning.

The door opened. My worst fears were realized. The pawnbroker and a policeman entered. To be short, I found I had made a great mistake in going to that pawn-shop where I was so well known, for it so chanced that the man I had robbed was the pawnbroker's nephew, — a young man from another State, on a visit.

As they entered, my mother raised herself in the bed, and pale as she was, I saw her cheek blanch.

My little sisters, trembling with a vague foreboding of disaster, caught each other's hands and edged close to her side.

I arose. I knew that the end had come.

" That is him — the villain! the young thief!" said the pawnbroker.

The officer advanced; he grasped me by the shoulder.

"I must arrest you, my man," he said; "you are charged with highway robbery!"

" That's it! that's it! the villain!" said the pawnbroker.

" Highway — robbery! Oh, God!"

It was my mother who gasped the words, and as the last one, uttered in a tone that cut me to the heart, escaped her lips, she fell back.

I dared not look at her.

" Ma! ma! oh, ma!" cried my sisters in an agonized voice, " oh, ma! don't die!"

" *Die!*"

The steel entered my soul. I felt, for a moment, like one struck suddenly with paralysis.

" Leave me!" I said hoarsely to the officer; " leave me, and take him out of the room. In a minute I will be ready, — I will go with you. Leave me alone for a minute with her, — with my mother. Leave me, will you?"

" No! no!" cried the pawnbroker. " He will run away."

The policeman, touched despite of himself, answered the cruel words with a look; then pointed to the door, and followed the pawnbroker out.

And then I was left alone; alone with my two weeping sisters, and what I had no doubt was the corpse of my mother.

I caught a sight of myself in the glass. My face was haggard, my lips white, my eyes stony.

For a moment I stood perfectly motionless. No words can describe the tumult of my feelings. I felt that I had been wronged; that the world had used me harshly. The fires of hell burned within my breast. In that one moment I went to the bad!

The little ones had ceased their cries and fallen suddenly into a deep sleep, and an oppressive silence reigned in the room.

I advanced to the bedside and gazed intently on the still, white face, so calm in its repose. A multitude of thoughts, too confused and indistinct for expression, surged through my mind. My heart was bursting with emotion, and my whole being thrilled with a nameless sensation.

She was dead, and she had been my mother. My mother — and I had never been able to provide her with the least luxury; I had never been able to give her one moment's peaceful rest. Others had been rolling in wealth, while we were starving.

I thought, then, of my father's last rash act. He had committed the crime out of love for us; he had meant to aid us, and he had worked our ruin. He made us the wife and children of a criminal, — a criminal who had been painted as guilty of the blackest ingratitude, for no one ever knew the truth, — and no one would trust us! Even when the employer would have retained us, there was a cry raised by the

15 *

employees against him. *They* could not afford to be contaminated by our presence.

Why, you may ask, had we not emigrated to some strange place where our history was unknown? Why? One word will answer the question: *money!*

Well, the end had come at last. *Her* troubles were all over. There was some happiness in that thought.

I bent over and kissed her cold, mute lips for the last, last time. My grief was driving me wild, and I had not a tear to relieve me.

"Mother! mother!" I cried, "I have been ambitious; I have tried to be great and good, but they would not let me. Now they shall feel my sting; now I shall be great and bad!"

I turned away. I had done forever with the old life. I said not a word to the little ones; I did not even murmur, "God help you!" I had ceased to believe in the power of God to help or save.

When the officer entered the room, he found me standing like a statue carved out of stone, but ready to go with him.

The next morning I learnt another lesson on the difference between being rich and poor. A rich *murderer* was driven in a carriage to the Court-House. How was it with me? Was I driven to the court-room? No! I, with others, was made to walk in the public street with manacles on my wrists, and followed by a gaping, curious crowd.

My eyes fell. Remember that this was my first experience in the ways of the transgressor. Remember that I was not a hardened criminal, dead to all shame. I felt the humiliation keenly. I said to myself, there is no use of my trying to be good now; everybody will know me.

That experience hardened me. Think of it! And remember, too, that some of my fellow-prisoners were innocent men! I could swear that after that day they became criminals.

Can you imagine any quicker, any surer way of deadening a man's feelings, of making him lost to all shame, of killing every finer sensibility of his nature, than by walking him manacled through the public street, with a gaping, grinning crowd at his heels?

My spirit revolted; I felt that it would be the acme of bliss to crush the entire world out of existence. I was ready for anything desperate! You will not wonder, then, that when I saw Crompton's face among the spectators behind me, and saw his eyes light up with demoniac triumph as they fell upon my countenance, I rushed quickly upon him, before my guardian, unaware of my purpose, could prevent me.

I was committed for trial. I was tried on two charges, one for highway robbery, and the other for assault and battery. I made no defence; it would have been useless to have made the attempt, when I had no witnesses to prove any facts I might have stated.

The judge kindly told me that I was a desperate villain, and that he owed it to the community to put me out of the way of doing harm for ten years. Oh, kind judge! most merciful judge! it's so easy saying "ten years." What do you know of prison life? Why, when a convict who killed a warden offered in his defence his treatment in prison, you refused to listen to a word. And then you thought him an utterly irredeemable villain, because, when you refused to hear his story, he sat down, invited you to sentence him to death, and laughed at the ceremony of the jury bringing in a verdict! You thought him heartless, because he said, " I don't consider that I have been tried yet, but I am perfectly satisfied with the result. To be hanged would be an act of supreme mercy, compared to being compelled to live in the State prison." *

Well, I went to the State prison, and assumed the convict's garb. Here I learnt another lesson on the power of money. If I had been rich, some light work would have been assigned to me. As it was, I was put at a kind of work for which I was utterly unsuited, both bodily and mentally speaking. My health at last failed me, and for weeks I hovered between life and death. I can't say that I received the best treatment. It mattered not whether the convict lived or died. In fact, if he died, it was so much the better.

When I recovered, I was placed in the shoe factory. Did I learn to make shoes? Was I taught any trade by means of which I could make an honest living when released from imprisonment? Not a bit of it! I was taught a special branch of the business, but I never learnt how to make shoes. I could no more have set up for a cobbler, than I could have soared.

I have to find great fault with the practice of teaching prisoners a special part of a work; for instance, what I was taught — cutting leather. It is not easy to secure a position requiring only this specialty. If a prisoner is expected to live honestly, upon his dis-

* The very words used.

charge, he should be taught a means of livelihood. If he is, to take my own case, put in the shoe department, he should learn the whole business, — how to make an entire shoe, not how to make a part. In short, he should be fitted for a regular cobbler.

The practice in the prison where I was confined was otherwise.

Prisons, you say, were made for purposes of reformation. They may have been made for such purposes, but they are not used for them. Take my own case again. I was a new convict; it was my first offence. Yet, instead of being confined in a separate place, I was huddled in with men hardened in crime; men who made light of every sin; who took the prison as one of the natural events of their lives; who intended, when they were released, to resume their law-breaking, but to be more careful in their operations, and not to be caught again, if they could help it.

. What could be the effect on me of this indiscriminate association? Could it do me any good? Was it likely to have a beneficial effect on my mind? Or was it not more likely to harden and deprave me—to kill whatever of the good remained in me? The poet wrote truly :

> Vice is a monster of so frightful mien,
> As to be hated, needs but to be seen ;
> But seen too oft — familiar with her face,
> We first endure — then pity — then embrace.

Oh ! I tell you, your prison system needs a thorough overhauling. An entire change in the method of treating criminals is needed, if you ever expect to work their reform. Your present system is radically bad.

M

Let me point out some defects in the State prison where I was confined. It was very improperly guarded. The keepers were men utterly unfit for the position. They were brutal, and they could do whatever they wished. They had full power to obey the promptings of their malice. If they took a dislike to a man, woe be to him. On the other hand, the rules of the prison were such that if a convict felt dissatisfied with anything, he could stop his work on the instant, and march to the warden with his complaint, regardless of the keeper's presence, instead of being compelled to wait until a regular hour set apart for the hearing of complaints by the warden. This was not calculated to inspire the convict with a sense of obedience to his keeper, and the latter had to rule through fear. Again, if the keeper denied a charge, the convict's complaint was, in nine out of ten cases, disregarded entirely. I admit that in many instances their complaints had no foundation in fact, and were groundless. But there were cases which came under my observation, — in one of which *I* was the complainant, — which demanded, and should have received, thorough investigation, but which were unheeded.

Again, by reason of the manner in which the prison was guarded, every inducement was placed in the convict's way to escape. There were too few keepers over too many men, and every temptation to endeavor to regain his liberty was placed prominently before the prisoner, so that he could not refrain from forming the idea. When one did make the attempt and failed, then he was punished, — punished for obeying the impulse of his nature—for being a human creature possessed of a human nature.

Well, my time came at last, and I was set at liberty.
Liberty! I had not known it for years, and my heart
beat wildly with the consciousness of freedom as I
stepped out of my convict's garb.

Evidently, however, I was expected to return before
long, for the last words — cheering words! — spoken
to me were:

"Good-bye. *We'll see you soon again.*"

You see experience had taught the officials that they
who stopped at the prison once, would be sure to return. A very good idea of the reformatory nature of
the institution they had!

But, leaving aside the effect of the life I led within
those walls, was it not natural that they should expect
me to return? Let me show you why it was so:

First. I knew no trade. I had not been fitted for
any business. I was not a cobbler, a carpenter, a
plumber, — in fact, I knew as little when I came out
as when I went in; I was just as ignorant of business;
I had as little experience to help me; I had nothing to
depend on.

Second. I had no place to which to go; no situation
of any kind awaiting me.

Third. My prison life had not been such as to inspire
me with the idea that I had been punished to teach me
that the way of the transgressor is hard, and that good
is preferable to evil. On the contrary, I had an indistinct idea that I had been persecuted, and that I
would be justified in revenging my wrongs on my
persecutor, viz., Society.

Fourth. I had but money enough to carry me to my
destination; I would arrive there penniless; I could

not secure any kind of work immediately; no provision was made for me until I could, if I desired, by search-ing, find a place; I would find myself homeless and starving; my mind was used to the idea of crime, and it followed, therefore, that I would not be so apt to hesitate and think over what I was doing, before com-mitting an offence against the law.

To proceed. I jumped aboard a city bound train. A passenger seated by my side — I wonder if he had known who I was, would he have changed his seat? — was reading a newspaper. I glanced over it. A name, Martindale, caught my eye, and riveted my attention instantly. I asked the stranger in a trem-bling voice if he would be kind enough to loan me his paper for a second. He did so; he did not know that I was a discharged convict. I seized the paper greedily. Imagine with what emotions I read this:

"A man was found dead in —— Street yesterday. Death had evidently resulted from starvation. De-ceased was worn almost to a skeleton. The body is believed to be that of John Martindale, a bummer around low groggeries. It now lies in the Morgue. An inquest will be held, and the body interred in Potter's Field."

The paper dropped from my hands. John, my brother! I had no doubt it was him. So, that was the end to which he had come! Died alone, homeless, friendless, starving! — died a death of shame and misery! A bitter oath escaped my lips, as I thought of it.

And my sisters? what had become of them? Were they alive or dead? If alive, *what were they?*

My brain was kept busy with the most horrible conjectures.

The train arrived at the depot, and I stepped off.
I was in the city again, for the first time in many long
years. Where should I go? To the Morgue! I
would go look at the corpse! I would make sure
whether it was John's or not. I remembered that in
boyhood he had printed the initials of his name on his
right arm, indelibly, with India ink.

As I walked through the streets, I could perceive
many changes and improvements which had been made
since last I had wandered along them. Everything
seemed strange to me. For the time being my attention was called away from myself.

At length, I reached the Morgue. I stopped a moment before entering, and a sense of my own hopeless
condition came over me ; a thought that I, some day,
might be brought here, flashed across my brain.

A little solemn-looking building of stone, with an
architecture of tomb-like severity outside, and grave
simplicity within, was the Morgue, — that receptacle
for the unknown dead yielded up by the river and
found in the street. They lie on slabs of marble, —
each on its narrow shelf laid out, — a tube curling over
from which a continuous spray of fresh water was
showered on the corpse. On a hook fixed directly
above the head of the deceased, the articles of clothing
which were on the body, when it came into the charge
of the authorities, were hung.

There was nothing pleasant in the sight; no redeem-
ing feature. The picture presented was painted in jet

16

black; there was not a single touch of white to relieve its sombreness.

The corpse of a woman,—a woman who had evidently been beautiful in life, — who had, doubtless,

> Rashly importunate,
> Gone to her death!

for they took her from out of the river,—occupied the first slab. It was easy to stand still for a moment and tell what her life had been. It required no vivid imagination to solve the mystery of her death; to read the misery of her life.

There was to me a sort of fascination in the sight of these friendless dead — in the endeavor to surmise the history of each of these unfortunates. At every slab I stood for more than a minute, and gazed intently on the corpse.

Number two was an old man. He had been found dead in the street, with a ghastly gash across his throat. I looked upon the poor body, but my thoughts were not of him, but of his murderer. Who was he? What had driven *him* into crime? Where was he? Was he wandering restlessly over the earth, a prey to fear and remorse, or was he just as happy, just as much at his ease, just as free in his mind, as though his hands had never been steeped in the blood of a fellow-creature?

Sentiment replied affirmatively to the first question; experience answered "yes" to the last.

Number three was a man. There was a small hole in his forehead, through which the fatal bullet had entered his brain. This was a case of suicide; cause, poverty! What misery he must have known, what privation and suffering he must have endured, before he committed the rash act which sent his body to the Morgue, thence to be conveyed to the grave of the friendless and destitute — Potter's Field! It was all over now; he was at rest. Perhaps this was the happiest hour he had ever known. Who could say?

The next was another case of suicide. A young man, whose features told plainly that he had belonged to the upper grade of society. Drink and debauchery had brought him here. Was any one mourning for him?

The last was the man I had come to see, — my brother. This corpse was all that remained of him.

"Oh, John! John!"

An official passing by stopped and looked at me. Perhaps, used as he was to such scenes, the agony in my voice touched him.

"Do you know him?" he asked.

I could not speak; I could not answer.

"Perhaps this may aid your memory," he said; "it was the only thing found in his pockets."

He handed me a small tin-type. It was the picture, faded somewhat, of a woman. It sent a thrill through me, for it was the picture of —

My mother!

Poor John! He had left us, doubtless, with some faint idea of coming back within a short time with the fruits of his secret labor to relieve our wants. And we had never seen him again! Why he had not returned, I would never know.

But he had never parted with this picture; he had cherished it always; he had died with it near him.

I could only say to the official that I would come
again on the morrow to claim the corpse; to be careful
of the picture, as I desired to bury it with the dead
man.   And then I left.

I was glad to get outside of the dead-house again.
I walked along, pondering deeply, my eyes bent on the
ground.   Suddenly, some one accosted me.

"Hello!"

I looked up with a start.   Before me stood a young,
fine-looking man, arrayed in the height of fashion.   I
recognized him.   He was a fellow-convict.   We had
taken a liking to each other while in the prison.   He
had been released a month previous to the expiration
of my time.

"How are you?" I exclaimed.   "How are you
getting along?"

"I'm well, and doing well," he replied.   "How
long have you been out?"

"Since this morning."

"And what are you going to do?"

"I don't know.   I must look for some situation."

"Situation?   Fudge!"   He was younger in years,
older in crime, than I was.   "Lord bless you!" he
continued, with a laugh, "how foolish you are!   Suppose you are asked for references,—you will be, sure,—
what will you do? refer to your last employer, the
State?   Pshaw!   You will never get along.   I have
tried it, I tell you!   I know what it is.   Just come
along with me, if you want to find out what it is to
live.   We'll get along first-rate together."

He used very potent arguments: they seemed to me
conclusive; he said a great deal to me with a serious-

ness of which I had not thought him capable. I need not repeat all he said. It ended in my going with him.

Two days afterward I was walking along Centre Street, when my attention was attracted to a crowd of urchins, following a policeman in charge of a woman. It was the most disgusting sight I have ever seen. Her dress was in rags, open at the bosom, falling off her back, and covered with dirt and vermin. She staggered along the street screeching snatches of a wild obscene song, her coarse, unkempt hair strewn down her forehead, her features distorted beyond recognition, her face bloated, and her expression fearfully repulsive. Even the policeman shrank away from her with an indescribable fear. Never, never have I seen a human being so inexpressibly loathsome.

The sight sickened me. I turned away. Shall I tell you who that wretched creature was? I found it out afterwards.

She was my sister — one of the little girls whom I had left sleeping the sleep of innocent childhood on the night of my arrest! * * * *

Let me make a retrospection.

My mother had not been, as I had imagined, dead. It proved to be only a faint.

On the day when I was sentenced, Crompton called on her. She was without a protector, and too ill to work, even had she had something to do. He repeated his offer. He pointed to her two little girls, — how were they to live? Thus he took advantage of a mother's love.

Sick, wearied, despairing, and desperate, she succumbed to him.

16 *

Unfortunately for her, he was thrown out of his carriage one day, a month afterwards, and killed. I think he would have provided for her had he lived; I will do him the justice to say this. As it was, she was left penniless. Worse, for even her reputation was lost now.

Let me be brief. She became a prostitute; the little girls grew up to enter upon the same living death. You start, Madame Society; you do not like that word prostitute. Let me tell you that prostitution is one of your greatest protectors. Unregulated, it is an evil, too; with proper regulation it becomes a protection only.

I have done. I have written more than I originally designed. It was my intention to show only how I came to take my first step in crime, and now I will close.

There is many and many a woman who, finding herself unable to make an honest living, or to procure honest work at something more than starvation wages, is listening to the voice of the tempter. There is many and many a starving child being reared in ignorance * and crime, being educated in the school of sin. And there is many and many a family, who, deprived of their natural supporter, shunned and pointed at as the

---

* A late report of the Commissioner of Education shows that there are 1,700,000 illiterate white youths and adults in the country, and another half million of children under ten growing up in ignorance. In 1860, according to the census, there were 346,893 illiterate adults of foreign birth, and 871,418 native born. There were in Pennsylvania, 36,000; New York, 20,000; Ohio, 41,000; Indiana, 54,000, etc. These figures, be it remembered, though as full as can be ascertained, necessarily fall *far* short of the truth.

wife and children of a criminal, unable to secure the necessaries of life, and rendered desperate by trouble, are drifting surely and rapidly into the ranks of the enemies of law and society. Who will save them? Who will rescue them before it is too late?

Oh! that there were some office under the law charged with the duty of caring for them. It is the law that has deprived them of their natural protector. It is *right* that the man who commits a crime should be punished. It is *wrong* that the innocent should be made to suffer for his crime.

Oh! I repeat, that there were some office under the law charged with the duty of caring for them; of aiding those who would, to emigrate to some new place, where, their history unknown, they could begin life anew; of seeing that the children were properly educated; that the wife, and those of the offspring who are able, were provided with suitable work, — for I do not ask the law to encourage idleness, — work by means of which they could earn an honest living, without feeling that they were dependent on charity, without feeling their pride hurt. For pride, of some kind or other, is the most natural and strongest feeling implanted in the human heart; pride, which will keep the greatest coward on the battle-field, and force him to be brave. If, perchance, there be a case found where the people refuse absolutely to work, there are the vagrant acts.

But it would be a waste of time for me to stop and elaborate the particulars of the plan I have in my mind. Though such an office, properly conducted, would, in a short time, become self-supporting, and even yield a revenue, I can see no prospect of its establishment.   Modern philanthropy consists in show; in the erection of grand buildings, egotistically called after the founder, for the approbation of the world; in asking the poor, in words of patronizing pity, to walk in, instead of *your* taking the trouble to find them out.   And yet you know well enough that the really poor are not the ones who go begging through the streets — are not the ones who go seeking after charity.   If they were, you would never have to read in your paper the words "Died of Starvation."

Listen!   The condition of the masses is growing worse and worse.   The spirit of Communism is spreading rapidly, and undermining the foundations of society — the spirit of Communism in its very worst form.   Unless some great change in the condition of mankind occurs soon, the world will wake some day to regret its neglect.   I can see a revolution approaching; I can see, though dimly, the change that is going to take place, — a change which may be effected by peaceable measures, but which is far more likely to be the result of a Social War, and the shedding of streams of human blood.   CHARLES WILTON.

P. S. Says Victor Hugo, "The three great problems of the age, — the degradation of man by poverty, the ruin of woman by starvation, and the dwarfing of childhood by physical and spiritual night, — are not solved."

I have cheated the gallows.   With my dying breath I swear that the paper which I executed before the jailer the other day is the solemn truth.   To the prison officials, who have treated me so kindly during my imprisonment, I return my sincere thanks, and also to the clergymen who would have consoled me in my last hours, and I ask their pardon for refusing to receive them.   All I can say is, that if I had received the same treatment in my youth that I have received during my imprisonment, I would never have been brought to this pass.   CHARLES WILTON.

That was all.   But, oh, what a scathing commentary upon society those last few words were!

"*If I had received the same treatment in my youth that I have received during my imprisonment, I would never have been brought to this pass.*" *

Philosopher! philanthropist! humanitarian!   Remember those words; they contain plenty of food for thought and reflection.   They were the last words of a criminal who knew what he was saying, who was conscious of their meaning.   They showed that he might have been made something other than he was. They said:

"*The way to prevent crime is not to punish the man, but to guard and look after the boy.*"

*   *   *   *   *   *   *

No one ever knew who it was furnished the murderer of poor, unfortunate Alice, with the means to commit his last terrible crime.   That was a secret which Mary Farly carried with her to the grave, and whatever suspicions the jailer might have had, he wisely kept them to himself.

Philip Marton's confession did not give the name

* The identical words used by a celebrated criminal.

14 *   L

of the person who had aided him in gaining an entrance to his victim's house. With that honor which is said to exist among thieves, he declined to reveal it.

True to the promise she had made him, Mary Farly allowed a year to elapse after his death before she made the true facts in relation to the murder of Leslie Wyndham public.

How they were received, and the surprise and excitement they created, can better be imagined than described. They carried with them the force of truth, and little by little other circumstances came to light, which proved conclusively the innocence of the unfortunate young man who had fallen a victim to popular excitement; yet, notwithstanding all this, there are many people living to-day who still continue to believe him guilty. The injury which the world has done to him can never be fully atoned for; the life they had taken it was impossible to return.

And now a few words more and we have done.

Most of the events which we have narrated had their origin in Mrs. Crosswell's house, between Leslie Wyndham, James Farly, and his wife, Mary. Who was to blame? Some of you will say the woman, for she did not do her full duty as a wife. Others will place the blame on James Farly, and some will be found who will blame Leslie Wyndham for interfering between them. As for ourselves, we might say one, we might say the other, and yet again we might say all three. However, we leave it to you to decide, only cautioning you to be careful how you judge, lest you, too, be IN FAULT.

THE END.

www.ingramcontent.com/pod-product-compliance
Lightning Source LLC
Chambersburg PA
CBHW020536270326
41927CB00006B/598